DORRY KORDAHI

POWER TO ACT

AN ENTREPRENEUR'S VISION

JoJo
PUBLISHING

www.powertoact.info

Power to Act
Dorry Kordahi

Published by JoJo Publishing
First published 2011

'Yarra's Edge'
2203/80 Lorimer Street
Docklands VIC 3008
Australia

Email: jo-media@bigpond.net.au or visit www.jojopublishing.com

© Dorry Kordahi Management 2010 – All rights reserved

All rights reserved. No part of this printed or video publication may be reproduced, stored in or introduced into a retrieval system, or transmitted, in any form, or by any means (electrical, mechanical, photocopying, recording or otherwise) without the prior written permission of the publisher and copyright owner.

JoJo Publishing

Editor: Julie Athanasiou
Designer / typesetter: Chameleon Print Design
Printed in Australia by Griffin Press

National Library of Australia Cataloguing-in-Publication data

Author: Kordahi, Dorry.
Title: Power to act : an entrepreneur's vision : opening your path
          to success / Dorry Kordahi.
Edition: 1st ed.
ISBN: 9780980619348 (pbk.)
Subjects: Kordahi, Dorry.
          Businessmen--Conduct of life.
          Success in business--Australia.
Other Authors/Contributors:
          Athanasiou, Julie.
          Santer, Lynn
Dewey Number: 650.1

The material in this publication is of nature of general comment only, and does not represent professional advice. It is not intended to provide specific guidance for particular circumstances and it should not be relied on as the basis for any decision to take action or not take action on any matter which it covers.

Readers should obtain professional advice where appropriate, before making any such decision. To maximum extent permitted by law, the authors and publisher disclaim all responsibility to any person, arising directly or indirectly from any person taking or not taking action based upon the information in this publication.

Contents

FOREWORD BY ZAIDEE JACKSON 1

CHAPTER ONE – HUMBLE BEGINNINGS 5
Entrepreneurial Strategies:
- Overcoming obstacles 10
- Own the circumstances in your life 10
- Set your goals and control your own destiny 11

CHAPTER TWO – CHILDHOOD DREAMS 15
Entrepreneurial Strategies:
- Prepare for success 23
- Remain grounded 24
- Learn from your role models 26

CHAPTER THREE – A BASKETBALL PLAYER?
A HAIRDRESSER? THE ENTREPRENEUR! 29
Entrepreneurial Strategies:
- Find your true calling 39
- Believe in yourself 41
- Learn from other people's mistakes 43

CHAPTER FOUR – DISCOVERING MY PURPOSE 47
Entrepreneurial Strategies:
- Recognise and reward staff 60
- Don't blur the lines between business and friendship 61
- Tips for starting out 63

CHAPTER FIVE – TURNING THE VISION INTO REALITY 67
Entrepreneurial Strategies:
- Taking risks sets you apart from the crowd ... 84
- Portray confidence 85
- Never give up 87

CHAPTER SIX – THE FLEDGLING 89
Entrepreneurial Strategies:
- Establish and build relationships with the best allies 99
- Hire young staff and train them in your image 102
- Keep it simple and don't overstaff 103
- Make your operation look as big as possible, without lying about it 105
- Compete for awards 108

Chapter Seven – Branded: Thinking Outside the Box 113
Entrepreneurial Strategies:
- Piggyback other distribution channels 117
- Think outside the box 119
- Don't aspire to the market standards — create your own and raise the bar 120

Chapter Eight – The Rebirth of an Idol 127
Entrepreneurial Strategies:
- Create your own benchmarks 139
- Be grateful and give back 140
- What doesn't kill you makes you stronger 140
- Branding is art, not science 142

Chapter Nine – The Sydney Kings 147
Entrepreneurial Strategies:
- Spend wisely 159
- Connect (leverage) your networks 160
- It's okay to have small goals and prepare for the down times 161
- Tough times call for smart measures 161

CHAPTER TEN – WHAT I'VE LEARNT ABOUT MERCHANDISING.. 165
   Entrepreneurial Strategies:
   - Brand quality is king 171
   - Don't settle for poor customer service 172
   - Get in early to get results 174

CHAPTER ELEVEN – THE POWER OF POSITIVE THINKING 177

Foreword

By Zaidee Jackson

We are all born with an inner ability to achieve, no matter what our goals. Whether it is setting personal goals for the short term or building a more secure financial future, there is a trigger within us all. For some that trigger is never set in motion; for others, the explosion of success takes on a life of its own.

As a friend of Dorry Kordahi for the past 18 years, it has been a pleasure to witness a remarkable transformation in him. Personally and professionally, there has been a single commonality: a clear desire, passion and hunger to achieve beyond anyone's wildest dreams. With its transparent approach, I am delighted that this autobiography shares his journey and secrets of success. I have always known Dorry as a man who doesn't hesitate to own his achievements. As Dorry puts it, "If I can do it, so can everyone else — everyone, that is, who wants it badly enough". When I asked what sustains him personally and professionally, he said simply, "My self-belief and maintaining my substance as an individual.

I am someone who cares about the repercussions of my decisions and actions".

At 34, Dorry exudes the charisma and confidence consistent with a young, successful entrepreneur but, at the same time, it is always apparent that he is grateful for his success.

"I can't afford to take my achievements and success for granted," he says. "My fulfilment comes from my love of what I do."

Once a towel boy at age 13 for the national basketball team, the Sydney Kings, Dorry eventually became a shareholder. With little knowledge of the music industry, Dorry began managing the career of one of Australia's rising artists, Cosima De Vito. Deliberately positioning himself in challenging situations is part of his formula to rise to ever more dizzying heights.

"I'm open to learning something new every day," he says. "That is what keeps me going. Not only on a professional level but also in the decisions I make in my personal life."

He has an innate ability to overcome obstacles that, for the most part, he himself sets.

"I expected to be successful; I wouldn't settle for anything less," Dorry states. "I wanted to define the term 'success'. Focus and vision are paramount to anyone's journey; however, attempting to achieve success without finding a balance can result in one heading in the wrong direction. There are so many ideas I would like to bring to fruition. I have learned that timing and planning are everything. The one thing of which I have no fear is working hard and staying focused."

A sentiment we both share is that, as individuals, our greatest asset in the journey to success is openness to learning. But Dorry has always possessed the knack of observing that extra something in a situation.

Working hard to achieve while believing in himself is the reason Dorry takes it all in his stride. Indeed, Dorry's journey has not always been clear-cut. Decisions were made through inexperience. Lessons were learned along the way. How those lessons were interpreted could have just as easily worked to his detriment instead of, as is now evident, to Dorry's benefit.

Who would we rather be: the scriptwriter, or the actor playing a part in someone else's play? Dorry chose from the outset to write his role in life. His dreams were brought to fruition and he continues to grow, to strive for and to achieve greatness in all that he does. Part of that desire is wealth, not as it relates to financial security but the wealth of being an individual who is proud to reflect on his achievements; wealth relative to the sound relationships he shares with his family and the healthy respect he has for others. I wish Dorry all the blessings of continued success along a grounded road, with the occasional twist to keep him growing and achieving.

To my family for their ongoing love and support.

Chapter One

HUMBLE BEGINNINGS

If I had been told at a young age that I would be successful at something I had been told I was bad at, I would have said, "No way". Well it's funny how the universe works and what it brings to you. Not many people would be ready to write their life story at 35 years of age but I feel I have something to share. While there is little doubt that, in many ways, I have been blessed, my achievements are something that anyone who takes a leaf out of my book can emulate.

In this book, I wish to share some insight into my background and how I got to where I am today. At the end of each chapter, I will summarise the lessons learned from each story, using my 'Entrepreneurial Strategies' to explain the points and examine certain aspects of the story. These are features of my story which I hope will add value to you and your vision.

Even as a young child, I had dreams and visions that were far beyond the horizons of my family's expectations. I believed — in fact I innately knew with the burning passion of certainty — that somewhere beyond the bounds of past experience I was going to become successful. But, before I was truly able to shine, I needed to find my purpose.

With no higher education or family fortune behind me and armed only with that burning desire to succeed, I proved that, by possessing the power to act, it's possible not only to reach the seemingly unreachable star but positively touch the lives of countless others along the way.

It is very important that you understand a few aspects of my makeup before you reach points in my story where you might say to yourself, "That could never happen to me".

Where there is light, there is also darkness. For the first time, in this book, I have freely and frankly revealed some of my darkest moments. This not only puts my triumphs into important perspective, it will also — and this is crucial for those of you who yearn to emulate my success but are intimidated by my seeming to possess a Midas touch or innate ability that cannot be taught — illustrate that no man can shine without shadows.

All too often, people view others who have exceeded their level of achievements with envy. They fail to see the undeniable truth: that anyone can realise their full potential if they are prepared to commit to their dream and accept that, where there are highs there are also lows. We may not glimpse the lows in those we admire (or envy) from afar but they are there. So, before you do anything else, make the commitment to see your

Chapter One | **Humble Beginnings**

vision through, no matter how bumpy the road may become.

My beginnings were unremarkable. Born to a middle class, close-knit family, I was raised with strong values. My mother stayed at home to take care of the family while my father earned a living. I wasn't brought up with wealth or the luxuries that money can buy. It was more about acquiring the values of respect, family and traditions. I see now that having those values kept me grounded and humble.

My father, Joseph, was a highly respected professional in his hairdressing trade. He honed his skills and refined his craft, always wanting to give his clientele the best value for their money. For nearly 40 years, he ran his own business, first by running two salons in Lebanon and, later, when they migrated to Australia in 1976, in Sydney. At 25 years of age, my father arrived in 'the lucky country' to make a new start with his family. He did not speak fluent English so he enrolled in an English language course. Following this, he secured a position at a salon in the Boulevard Hotel on William Street in Sydney. Within three months, he saw an opportunity to open up a salon in the suburb of Punchbowl. Even now, as a retired gentleman, he still coifs the odd client, although these days it is more of a hobby.

Two of my younger siblings were born in Australia, my brother, David and my sister, Christine. My older brother,

Danny and I were migrants along with our parents; I was only a year old. So what made my parents uproot our family and travel across the world with two toddlers to start a new life in a country where they could barely speak the language? War.

The civil war broke out in Lebanon in 1975. My aunt left her homeland almost as soon as the first shots were fired and it didn't take my dad long to follow suit. Eventually, my father's entire extended family left their ancestral homeland to settle in a climate where it felt safer to raise their children. They could just have easily gone to France or elsewhere in Europe but Australia was seen as the land of opportunity by many and enthused about my aunt who had migrated to the land down under a few years earlier. The Kordahi family believed there were more opportunities in this brave new world than anywhere else they might have chosen to migrate. Not everyone was fortunate enough to pack up and leave behind the violence erupting all around them. My mother, Mary, left her whole family behind.

I admire my dad, Joseph and give him a lot of credit for uprooting his wife and two young children to start over in a new country with little money and limited English at such a young age. To have the drive and determination to open up a salon within his first year is something I greatly respect. Nothing I experienced could rival what my father put on the line for his family to ensure we were raised in a safe society.

Back then, the area of Punchbowl was quite raw but, even so, setting up a new business took money. With only a couple of thousand dollars to his name, my father secured a loan from his sisters, who were convinced that he would build a solid reputation for himself in his new country. Had he remained in Lebanon, our family's financial security would likely still have been assured, as my father possessed strong political connections which no doubt would have taken him a long way. However, financial security is no substitute for physical and emotional security, so he was prepared to forsake material comfort for the love and safety of our family. For my father and, in turn, for me in emulating my father's morality, family is more important than money. Money comes and goes but family roots remain.

One of my more vivid memories as a small child was my first day at school. I remember kissing my mother goodbye and running into class. I was excited as this was something completely new. As I sat in class playing with some blocks, many of the kids around me were crying. I overheard the teacher comforting them, saying, "Don't cry. Look at Dorry. He is having fun playing". I can see now that this was an early indicator of my character. I did not fear the unknown then and I embraced new challenges. Looking at the person I am now, that moment likely defined who I was. We are all born with individual traits as human beings, but it's how we develop them that affects who we become.

Entrepreneurial Strategies – Chapter One

- Overcoming obstacles
- Own the circumstances in your life
- Set your goals and control your own destiny

Overcoming obstacles
"Life's ups and downs provide windows of opportunity to determine your values and goals. Think of using all obstacles as stepping-stones to build the life you want." — **Marsha Sinetar**

Everyone encounters obstacles in their lives but it is how willing and how determined we are to overcome obstacles that differentiates between those who succeed and those who don't. My biggest challenge was to face that fear of the unknown when starting my own business. We all have challenging moments in life, but, again, it's how you overcome those obstacles mentally that makes the difference. All hurdles can be cleared in some manner if you understand there is a purpose to them and that there are lessons to learn in every challenge you face.

Own the circumstances in your life
Accept responsibility for who you are and acknowledge your own strengths and weaknesses. You are the only person responsible for your success. If you believe in yourself and you believe in your vision, then don't hesitate.

There is a saying, "You don't land on a mountain; you climb a mountain". Some days will bring obstacles. How you rise above those obstacles is what sets you apart. It is what drives you to climb beyond those days and make them count.

Some fear it's egocentric to accept our own strength, as though demonstrating a natural ability is in some way exalting ourselves over others. It is not. If you have a gift, whether it is in sales, music, art, networking, embrace it and use it. It's all right to be quietly proud of it.

Conversely, some of you may not find it easy to accept yourself for who you are. All of us have things we dislike about ourselves. To survive, we must focus on the positives and shrug off the negatives. As long as you're happy with your choices, that's the only thing that ultimately matters.

Accepting yourself for who you are does not mean that you can't and shouldn't strive to make enhancements. What it does mean is that you are positioned perfectly from a point of strength to demonstrate the *Power to Act*.

Set your goals and control your own destiny

Success in any realm requires vision and goal-setting. In business, for example, there's no rule that says viable ideas must be accompanied by a 50-page business plan. My business plans were three pages of scribble! Not all business plans are the same, or need to be the same. The plan may differ in formula or structure. The imperative part is to implement it. If you don't implement it, then it has no value. So, the Power to Act is to move beyond verbalising the intent to implementing it, to where you actually *do it*. There are many people who spend so much time talking about what they are going to do that they never make time to do it!

That said, I always maintain, don't jump the gun. Although you may have an exciting idea or concept, you must first analyse it, you must visualise it. Assess the negatives in your chosen business and if you believe you can overcome the negatives mentally, then go for it! However, if you can't work through all the negatives in your head, revisit your thought process. Not all ideas are automatically viable. Working through the pros and cons is the first step to ascertaining whether or not you should move forward and spend further energy on your idea. That's a smart approach in business. If I can't consciously work through those negatives, then I don't proceed with an idea.

In terms of setting your goals and controlling your own destiny, well, this is in your hands. It's up to you what you choose to do with your destiny. Believe in yourself, work through the possible negatives and then follow through.

Notes

Chapter Two

CHILDHOOD DREAMS

It might appear as if I was no more than an ordinary migrant boy attending an ordinary school in an ordinary suburb. However, life is full of twists and turns that open up challenges, if our eyes are open to see them. Each and every decision we make has a ripple effect on whatever happens to us from that moment on. Even the most minor incidents can play out in ways that are unforeseeable. How many times have we heard of instances where a coincidence irrevocably changes a life? For example, perhaps a temporary delay in traffic resulted in someone avoiding an accident. Or someone who is angry because they missed their flight later discovers that the plane tragically crashed.

Coincidences can go either way and, more often than not, it seems too far-fetched to believe such links in the chain are anything but mere coincidence. But what is coincidence? Isn't it two incidents coinciding or perhaps even colliding?

What are the odds that a schoolboy who worked as a towel boy for a championship basketball team would later end up part-owning that team? Perhaps akin to a lightning strike? Well, not in my world, they're not!

I attended Holy Innocent Primary School in Croydon, followed by De La Salle College in Ashfield. Always a keen athlete, I played a variety of sports, including soccer and basketball until my father insisted I had to limit myself to one. My older brother selected basketball. I decided to do the same. If my older brother had selected soccer, I likely would have chosen soccer, too and an entirely different set of circumstances would have unfolded. But he didn't. We didn't. Basketball would become a passion, one that took me on an odyssey around the globe.

I played basketball for many years, progressing through the ranks to where I was selected to play for several All-Star teams while still a junior. I continued on to play State League and in the ABA (Australian Basketball Association) and participated in a few Sydney Kings' summer camp programs.

My friend's father was the manager of the newly formed Sydney Kings in 1988. I used to hang around with my friend helping the team by putting towels and singlets up in the change rooms for the players. From there I became one of the towel boys, wiping the sweat off the court during games.

Chapter Two | **Childhood Dreams**

As a 13-year-old, being involved with a professional team was intoxicating. To be around star players opened my eyes to the possibility of sport as a profession.

My progression through the junior ranks was memorable. I enjoyed playing Division One in my age group. My experience throughout this time is one I always fondly recollect.

An opportunity presented itself just as I was finishing my under 18's season. The next step typically was the Youth League (under 21's). Instead, I decided to try out for the Open Men's Division One team. I read about the tryout at the gym and I told Danny, my older brother, that I was going. He laughed and said I was too young to make it. That spurred me on! It might seem relatively minor but it had a major impact on my career at a young age.

I tried out with Tahi Martin, who's still a friend of mine today. Tahi was a year older but technically still too young for the men's team. Nonetheless, we gave it our best and, after three weeks of tryouts, the coach, Greg Jones, called us back. Neither of us knew if he'd tell us we'd been kidding ourselves or whether the coach had been impressed with our ability, but we were excited to have been called back together. To our amazement, Coach Jones wanted to put us in the first grade pre-season Division One Men's Team. It was arguably my life's most thrilling moment to date, my first real achievement as a young adult. To this day I can't recall the moment without a smile on my face. To be selected at such a young age to play for the men's team was a dream!

We played in the pre-season and after that we'd either have to roll down to our respective Youth League team or play in the State League senior team. We would train for four hours a night, two hours with the Division One team and two hours with the Youth League team.

Focusing so much on basketball, it's no wonder I failed my academic exams. I trained for four hours, three nights a week. However, despite all the training, dedication and perseverance and having played on the Division One Men's team, I was informed that I wasn't good enough to make the Youth League team.

I was floored. I was completely gutted. Didn't they realise I'd been playing Division One with the seniors? It's just not possible I could fail to make the Youth League team, I fumed. I stormed out of the gym. My first call was to my Division One coach, Greg Jones. He advised me not to worry about it and said I could continue to play with the seniors in the State League. I was mollified but it did not abate my anger with the other coach.

I have since learnt that every obstacle is a challenge to test the level of hunger and commitment in one's life, to reveal how determined one is to persevere and continue on one's journey. It is far better to turn a negative into a positive and to remember that all things happen for a reason in order to increase the chances of a better outcome in life.

Chapter Two | **Childhood Dreams**

The opportunity for me to remain in the State League program gave me the chance to travel through many small, country towns and experience what life on the road was like. At the time, I was one of the youngest kids to play in the State League program.

In our first home game, there was 0.7 seconds left in the game when a teammate was fouled out. The coach told me to get out there. I couldn't believe he was serious. I was still wearing my tracksuit over my uniform and felt foolish going onto the court for such an insignificant amount of time. I whipped off my track pants and track top and was on the court for no more than a snap of a finger before the game was over. That was my first taste of playing with the big boys. Instead of being excited, I felt humiliated. But no one else paid much attention and I swallowed my ego. Four or five games into the season, my on-court minutes started clocking up and I began averaging around 20-plus minutes a game.

One road trip we headed to Wagga Wagga and then Albury. We played in Wagga on a Saturday. The Wagga team was in last place, so I figured I could count on getting a generous amount of court time to increase my game experience. Instead, I barely got ten minutes that game, even though we were up by 40-plus points. I was frustrated. I knew the next day would be a far tougher game against Albury, currently in first place. Figuring I wouldn't see any play time, that night I went out with a few of the team supporters and didn't return to the hotel until 6:30AM. I sneaked back into the room and dived into my bed with my clothes on just as the coach was calling everyone for breakfast. Had he seen me sneak in, he likely would have suspended me for a few games.

Since I'd assumed I wasn't getting any court time against the top team, I wasn't too concerned. However, as luck would have it, several of our starting five got fouled out and I ended up playing more than thirty minutes that game. It was one of the toughest games I'd ever had to play, trying to conceal the side effects of the night out from my coach. I couldn't wait for the game to end. We lost. I learned a hard lesson, how important it is to be prepared at all times for any eventuality and never to assume anything as we never know what lies ahead.

Midway through the season I grew confident that I'd become an important part of the team. Yet, even then I couldn't shake off the anger at recalling how I'd been told I wasn't good enough to make the Youth League. There were politics involved. It was an important life lesson to be made aware of such machinations, for they happen in every facet of life. Politics are indeed everywhere.

Someone who still remains a big part of my life and who taught me a valuable lesson, one for which I will be forever grateful, is Leon Trimmingham. Leon was one of my closest friends growing up. We met on the very first day he set foot in Australia. I was shooting around at the Sydney Kings' training facility with my brother when Leon walked in, straight off the plane and was put

Chapter Two | Childhood Dreams

on the court for training drills. He looked pretty average on the court to my eye. I remember commenting to my brother that there was no way the Sydney Kings would keep him.

After his workout, I chatted with Leon and offered to show him around town. From that day, we forged a friendship which still stands strong today. I quickly changed the way I felt about Leon's game as he proved himself beyond a doubt one of the best imports the National Basketball League (NBL) has had to date. He is remembered for his amazing ability to jump over defenders. In my opinion, Leon is one of the most athletic players I have ever witnessed and his performances definitely changed my first impression that he wasn't good enough to compete in Australia.

I viewed Leon as a big brother. He was 23 years old and I was 18. We went everywhere together. There I was, a hairdresser on my $150-a-week salary, harbouring the ambition to one day play for the Sydney Kings alongside Leon. Leon became my inspiration. I would often tell him I was living my dream vicariously through him. Even the fans would ask to take photos of me with Leon and mistakenly ask for my autograph. I wasn't the star but I sure enjoyed the attention. When Leon left Sydney to play for Adelaide, it was a sad time for me. My closest friend was leaving to play in another state. Leon, though, would fly me out to Adelaide where I would spend weeks living and training with him. At one point he suggested I move to Adelaide, that he would pay for everything. I was sorely tempted. After all, what an amazing life I would surely lead. However, something made me hesitate. My pride wouldn't permit me to live my dream through someone else's eyes. I wanted to achieve success on my own. I respected Leon's friendship too much to ever take advantage of it in that way. The day might come when he'd be offered a position overseas and I just couldn't see me carrying his suitcases. It was great to enjoy the experience but I knew I couldn't afford to get lost in someone else's life or I'd lose focus on what I needed to do for myself. I was blessed to have such an amazing adolescence. I congratulate myself now for being able to recognise how my life could have turned out, had I focused on someone else instead of myself. Fortunately, I realised I had to focus on my goals. Today, Leon and I still keep in touch and look back on our earlier times together as a wonderful chapter in our lives.

Entrepreneurial Strategies – Chapter Two

- Prepare for success
- Remain grounded
- Learn from your role models

Prepare for success

To maintain success you must have the right mental approach. When you think about building a business, you must believe it can succeed and look at all the things that will accompany that success. It might be money. It might be fame. It might be more people wanting to befriend you.

I've seen it time and time again. People who become successful too quickly are often unprepared for everything that comes with it. They end up blowing money on unhealthy purchases and then turn around and think, "Where did all my money go?"

Mental preparation is a critical component to maintain success and definitely one where it helps to learn from other people's mistakes rather than just your own.

There is no escaping it, once you start climbing the ladder of success, people's attitudes towards you will change. You cannot control this but you can control how you react to it. This comes from confidence, not arrogance and by that I mean confidence in yourself and the path you have chosen.

All other things being equal, self-confidence is often the single ingredient that distinguishes a successful person from someone less successful. Make a clear promise to yourself that you are absolutely committed to your journey. No matter how others change around you, maintain your focus and continue to do everything in your power to achieve your goals. If doubts start to surface, take a deep breath. Analyse and challenge those doubts calmly and rationally. If the issues dissolve under scrutiny, that's wonderful. However, if the issues are based on genuine risks, make sure you set additional goals to manage them appropriately.

Either way, make that promise!

Remain grounded

Success is a wonderful thing to achieve, but sometimes it can be difficult to deal with. Living in the fast-paced, high-tech world of today can make it difficult to retain your inner happiness while striving to achieve. Many important aspects of your personal life can get lost in all of the excitement. I believe if you are humble and try to do good things with your success, then good will come back to you. It's called reaping what you sow.

There are fundamental steps to help deal with success well. Here are five to consider.

Step 1: Keep your feet on the ground. It's very easy to get caught up in your success and become so full of yourself that you feel you are above others.

Step 2: Let your accomplishments speak for themselves. When you gain your success, you won't need to tell everyone how successful you are. It will be evident to others without you saying a word.

Step 3: If your beginnings were modest, remember where you came from and who you are. Money has a way of changing a personality. If you have been fortunate to have been raised to be humble, do your best to remain that way.

Step 4: Live for the future, not just for today. It would be a big mistake if you only lived for today and spent unwisely, instead of investing in your future. Formulate a prospectus, a detailed outline of your future in order to deal with success. There will come a day when you will want to retire and, unless you have prepared a plan, you may find yourself having to make more sacrifices than you ever imagined.

Step 5: Spend quality time with friends and family. This is arguably one of the most important steps of all. Family and friends are the people who will support you the most. Success can often breed huge egos and arrogance, which can strain an otherwise good relationship.

Keeping good people around you, who really love you, will keep you grounded. Success attracts a lot of people who will sing your praises and not always with your best interests at heart. Be wise in your choice of friends and companions.

A true friend in triumph may be even harder to find. It takes tremendous loyalty for a friend to watch us soar when we are flying high rather than drag us back down. Loyal friends not only lend a hand when you're in need; they applaud your successes and cheer you on without envy when you prosper.

Learn from your role models

People often ask me who my role models are. My answer? Everybody. I'm a sponge, absorbing ideas from everyone I meet.

When I was younger, I spent a lot of time with people who were a lot older than me. I loved how successful they seemed. They could have been a national sales manager or anyone I thought at the time had a high position — I was determined to learn from their success. Today, in that capacity, I suppose I have become a role model myself. Yet, no matter how successful you are or how wealthy you become, you never stop learning from other people.

When we model ourselves after those who have achieved greatness, we try to adopt their character, their strengths and their determination. Their success can lead to our success and in the process we better ourselves. It's a win-win proposition.

Role-modelling is an effective and powerful step to achieve success. It provides us with inspiration and encourages us to move beyond temporary limits and failures. It also stimulates the creative imagination and draws from the subconscious mind ideas and insights, which might not otherwise come were we not so inspired. Let us not forget the most important principle of all. Your thoughts create your reality. Your mindset — what you think about and choose to dwell upon — imprints itself indelibly on your subconscious, particularly if you reinforce it through repetition each and every day. In this way, you can imprint the qualities of your mentors within yourself. So select your heroes and role models wisely and let them lift you to heights you might not accomplish on your own.

One caveat: I don't believe in copying people directly. I prefer to carefully observe what others whom I admire do, to learn not just from their successes but also from their failures. You don't want to lose your own identity in the quest to emulate. You need to create your own identity. Take from lessons learnt and emulate that which will make your journey a successful one.

Notes

Chapter Three

A Basketball Player? A Hairdresser? The Entrepreneur!

Although everything I've touched in later life may appear to have turned to gold, that was not always the case. In fact, as a child and in my early adult years, it seemed that everything I touched broke!

I had finished 12 years of school, albeit failing my High School Certificate with terribly bad marks. Considering I spent no more than a few minutes studying before each exam, it didn't come as any great surprise. I failed to apply myself at all to my studies. Like some kids, going to school was not a motivation. The only reason I persevered through to Year 12 was my desire to play basketball. Today, people who haven't seen me in 15 years still associate me with my passion for playing basketball. More often than not I am asked if I still play. I never really studied. The funny thing is, when I look back through my reports, many teachers wrote, "If only he applied himself, he would do well".

Looking back now, I find those comments intriguing and think, "Wow, they must have seen something in me that I didn't see myself".

Clearly, there was some spark of achievement potential, one capable of being either fanned or dowsed. I just wasn't paying attention.

Back then, my school was lauded for its sporting excellence. The role of star player on the basketball court came with special privileges, privileges I quickly identified and upon which I capitalised. I realised I could get away with pretty well anything I wanted. If I didn't want to attend a class, all I had to do was to go to my coach's office, sit down and talk basketball tactics. The coach would then scribble a letter excusing me from the class. Talk about being dealt a pretty easy hand! Using basketball as my excuse, I even managed to wriggle out of other sports classes. I was required to choose an alternative sport during basketball's off-season. I chose ice skating. I couldn't skate to save my life.

After only a few attempts, I was getting nasty blisters on my feet. I hated every moment of it. Instead of persevering or finding an alternative, I went to my Physical Education master and claimed that ice skating was bad for my ankles and would likely have an adverse affect on my basketball game. The solution? I was given Thursday afternoons off. I would finish classes at one o'clock and simply go home. Again and again, through a combination of being a sports star within our school

Chapter Three | A Basketball Player? A Hairdresser? The Entrepreneur!

and having a cheeky persona I got away with far more than I should have.

This was my first taste of favouritism. And it tasted great! I remember once being held back in detention during the first weeks of year seven and ordered to write lines for forty-five minutes in class. As luck would have it, the person supervising detention that day was my older brother's basketball coach.

When detention was over, the teacher announced that he was collecting the lines from everyone in the class. As he moved past each desk, he neglected to collect my pages. When he was finished, he announced that he was throwing away all the papers. He added that he wanted the lines re-written at home and on his desk by the next morning and dismissed the class. As the coach had not collected my work, this meant I could turn in my paper without having to do it all over again that night. At first I wondered if the oversight had been accidental, but I had sat in the middle of the room and he had collected everyone else's papers around me.

I didn't know whether to feel bad because I'd escaped the extra punishment, or feel good because of it. I decided to feel good! I was quite prepared to take any good fortune that came my way. I was spoiled — and I liked being spoiled. Even then, I knew this sort of preferential treatment would be easy to get used to.

However, nothing could magically improve my exam results. My grades were poor, I received a grade of 16 percent in Legal Studies, 26 in Maths and I failed Religious Studies — in a Catholic school! There was only one subject I didn't fail. Although I neglected my studies, ignored my teachers and never paid attention, I somehow passed my Business Studies exams. I just seemed to have a natural knack for business. I loved business and because I enjoyed what I was doing and was naturally inclined towards it, I succeeded in it. My parents were neither surprised nor disappointed with my abysmal results. It was assumed I would follow my father into the hairdressing business and there was little in my formal studies that would be of much benefit. Even if I had passed with flying colours, I was still expected to follow in my father's footsteps and join the family business. From Year 10 onwards, my teachers made their disappointment evident, especially those who saw the potential lurking beneath the surface of this wayward student. I have no regrets, although I'd never encourage anyone else to ignore the importance of school. I'm convinced that my story played out the way it was intended and I choose to continue to move forward past any obstacles, ensuring that the lessons have been learnt and not repeated.

I am a firm believer that, no matter what you may achieve in school, the experiences outside of your academic arena are also vital to groom you for the future. I feel fortunate to have been exposed to plenty of life's lessons through my sport and, as a result, found myself more open to identifying opportunities when they arose.

Chapter Three | A Basketball Player? A Hairdresser? The Entrepreneur!

Most of my fellow students weren't exposed to the things I was and therefore only saw life through the blinkers that the establishment insists upon. No doubt there are plenty of parents who might want to tear their hair out reading about my antics during my school years, particularly as, despite them, I went on to achieve success.

History is studded with examples of notable role models who flunked high school. Michael Jordan was cut from his high school basketball team; even Albert Einstein struggled at school. This is not intended to denigrate the value of a formal education, or to encourage anyone to drop out of his or her studies merely because some past success stories didn't start with a sound academic background. A sound education can provide a platform for a future with greater possibilities. I speak individually of my own personal experiences merely to give you a better understanding as to how and why I chose the direction in which I took my life. The fact is that I did indeed flunk high school, yet succeeded without any formal education. In hindsight, I believe my lack of formal education may have enabled me to overlook the risks and enhanced my professional outlook. Eventually with my business I was successful because I created a fresh approach. I've dealt with lots of people with degrees and most of them think the same way. They have all been taught to think inside the box when it comes to concepts like marketing. My lack of educational structure permits me to think outside the box because I was not taught what the box actually is.

Of course, being closely involved with sporting individuals and mixing with people older than me exposed me to risks that could easily have led me down a path of destruction. From the age of 16, I was hanging out in nightclubs with people many years my senior and that is when I first witnessed the destructive force of illicit drugs.

Common sense took hold, thankfully. Never was I tempted to experiment. It boiled down to possessing a strong sense of who I was. Exposure to that lifestyle can very easily lead you down the wrong path. I know now that I was hanging around with the wrong crowd but, even so, I never succumbed to undue influence. For this, I thank my parents. They taught me to believe in myself first and foremost, so I never felt the demands of peer pressure as kids so often do. If I become a father some day, I will endeavour to instil in my children that same strength and core belief that my parents instilled in me. Integrity is the foundation of character and is necessary to accomplish goals with strength, conviction and dignity. Giving in to peer pressure can be seen as taking the easy way out. Standing up for one's own beliefs in the face of such peer pressure is the lesson we all ideally learn and pass on to our children.

As I said previously, aside from my burning desire to play basketball, it was taken for granted that I would,

Chapter Three | A Basketball Player? A Hairdresser? The Entrepreneur!

upon leaving school, work in my father's hairdressing business. There was no real discussion about it. I was no scholar. I displayed no desire to go to university or college, so it seemed the only thing to do. My father wanted me to take over the family business. After four years, I received my apprenticeship and worked as a hairdresser from the age of 17 to 21. Thinking back now, it is hard for me to reconcile the person I am today with the one who spent his days in a salon, cutting and styling hair.

Hairdressing as a career wasn't for me although I wasn't half bad at it. It doesn't take a degree in clinical psychology to understand that hairdressing lacked appeal for a young man with big dreams. I wasn't driven by it so, like school, I didn't apply myself. However, I did make some effort for my family's sake.

Despite my father's initial frustration and disappointment, today he couldn't be happier that I chose the path I did. Instead of spending my days without passion, I elected to pursue my dreams. When I was shampooing and cutting, I dreamt about making money — serious money. I wanted the nice house, the nice car and, most of all, the freedom to be myself and to be respected for being that person. Every day I would visualise myself having these things that I wanted so badly. I knew in my heart that if I could see it, then I would make it happen. Today that may seem passé with the saturation of such publications as *The Secret*. Remember, however, that this was more than a decade before the publication of that book and such creative visualisations were, to my knowledge, far from commonplace.

I didn't know how I was going to do it or how I was going to get there but I knew I *was* going to get there. I knew that, if I could achieve it mentally and subconsciously, then I could make it happen physically. I'm living proof of that now.

I agree that no man is an island and, again, I credit my family upbringing for instilling within me high moral standards and discipline. (Well, except in school studies!) I credit my family for moulding my character and beliefs. While I was growing up, I yearned for the finer things in life, to achieve success, yet they were intangible — I wasn't even sure how to define those things.

During my hairdressing days I decided to get a Visa card with a $1,000 limit. I don't know how I managed to get such a limit on my weekly income of $150. I was excited and thought I could buy things even if I didn't have the cash to pay for it. Little did I know that the interest was mounting on my easy spending. I struggled to pay the card off but luckily for me my Dad came to the rescue. He paid off the debt, which was around $800. He then told me to cut the card and not to use it again. From that day onwards, I have never put myself in debt and realised a very important lesson: if you don't have the funds don't spend it. I was fortunate enough my Dad was there and I made sure I learned from this experience.

Chapter Three | A Basketball Player? A Hairdresser? The Entrepreneur!

As one of the best basketball players in the world, Michael Jordan was a hero to me. I watched documentaries about him where he stated, "I just knew I would be the best at what I did". Even when he didn't make his college team, he said he always knew eventually he would be the best in the world. When I heard that, it resonated. I was determined to reach my goals. I didn't realise it at the time but what I took away from those documentaries was a motto I live by every day now: to believe in myself. I always believed I would have what I wanted, even if I didn't know how I was going to get it. I didn't even know what my calling was; I just trusted that I would find it.

Therein lies what I hope every reader will take away from my story: believe in yourself and nothing is impossible. If you don't know what it is yet that inflames you with passion, don't wait until you discover it to begin believing in yourself. Start believing in yourself now and the rest will follow. Visualise your success, your achievements and trust that the path will appear before you. Remember the message of chapter one, to always be alert for opportunity. Having faith in yourself will enhance your awareness of life's chances. Visualise all the trappings that go along with the success you desire. See yourself driving that dream car — inhale the scent of that new leather; admire the colour; notice all the people marvelling at your vehicle as you drive by.

I had a number of false starts before I discovered what my true calling was but my end vision was always clear. At first, I assumed I'd be a hairdresser. Later, I was convinced I would be a star basketball player. In both cases I was wrong. Only now, standing on the other side, can I see how true and how powerful that belief in oneself is and how empowering the visualisation of owning one's dream can be. Picture the end result and you'll find the road to take you there.

So, you ask, how did I begin to connect the dots?

Entrepreneurial Strategies – Chapter Three

- Find your true calling
- Believe in yourself
- Learn from other people's mistakes

Find your true calling

Look around you. How many of the people you know are unhappy in their work and dissatisfied with their lot? This is because they have never sat down and dealt honestly and openly with themselves. We all have some form of inner talent and ability; the key is to recognise it, to identify it and use it. People enter the work force often like automatons, doing work that other people design. Their goals are those that other people have set. Is it any wonder then that, over time, these people who are not following their true callings begin to feel helpless? They feel that there is nothing they can do to change things because they're waiting for someone else to tell them how to change things. Their income only rises commensurate with their expenditure.

Your aim in life should be to become everything you are capable of becoming, to enjoy full self-expression of your talents and abilities. Your job is to develop yourself to the point where every day is a source of joy and satisfaction. Success comes from excelling at what you do and it's difficult to excel if you have no passion. The market rewards excellent performance with excellent compensation. Average performance yields average compensation. Below-average performance generates nothing more than below-average compensation. Which would you prefer?

It's important to note that excellence is a lifetime journey, not a destination. You don't get there and then get to relax. If you do, it will slip out of your grasp. The only thing that doesn't change is change. What constitutes excellence today will be different tomorrow and very different next year and the year after. Just look at the steady progress of technology if you don't believe me. You cannot rest on your laurels!

The joy in finding your true calling is that nothing but the best will do from that moment on. You will go any distance, pay any price and overcome any obstacle to obtain the excellence you now desire so passionately. You will drive yourself with that excitement, to begin the day a little earlier, work a little harder, stay a little later.

Over the years, people continue to wonder what they can do to be more successful. In almost every case, they are working in jobs that they don't like, for bosses they don't particularly respect, producing or selling products or services to customers they don't care about. They convince themselves that, if they just hang in there a little longer, the clouds will part and everything will get better. Pretty passive attitude, isn't it? You are where you are and who you are because of the choices you have made. Nobody can change your situation for you. If you don't have the drive and desire to excel at what you're doing now, it's likely you're in the wrong profession. It's time to look within.

Believe in yourself
To be successful, you must believe in yourself. You must have faith that your theories and your philosophies are right. But how do you know what is right and what is wrong? It's not as difficult as it might sound. What works for you, works for you. Many individuals start up companies in unorthodox ways; there's no right or wrong way.

If you have something you believe in, just do it.
- Don't base your life on the expectation of others. What you expect of yourself is often a higher goal and far worthier of your focus.
- If you need to write a business plan, to find investors or sell a business, just do it. Do it the way you need it to be done. Don't get bogged down thinking that you need to dress a certain way to fit into a meeting, or that the business plan must be 50 pages to be impressive. You define the parameters.
- If you are in a start-up business, think as an individual. Keep fast your convictions. If you imitate other people because you feel you must, then you've traded in your individuality, what sets your business apart, just to fit in and be like everyone else. Having done things my own way, I know this to be true. So, believe in yourself and follow through with your dream in your own way.

There may be days when you wake up to discover things aren't the way you had hoped they would be. That's when you have to tell yourself that things will get better. There are times when people disappoint you and let you down. But those are the times when you must remind yourself to trust your own judgements and opinions, to keep your life focused on believing in yourself. There will be challenges to face and changes to make in your life and it is up to you to accept them. Keep constant in the direction you know is right for you. It may not be easy at times but in those times of struggle you will find a stronger sense of who you are. So, when days come that are filled with frustration and unexpected responsibilities, remember to believe in yourself and all you want your life to be, because these challenges and changes are what can hone your drive, to attain the goals that you know are true for you.

Try these techniques to succeed in whatever field you choose:

- Learn how to make decisions based on your experiences. If you don't make your own decisions, you will never be truly successful.
- Set goals. When you set goals, you establish control.
- Recognise and celebrate when you achieve each goal. It will build your self-confidence.
- Consider the reasons you failed but don't punish yourself for them. Everyone experiences failure from time to time. If you learn from it, you are that much more likely to succeed the next time.

*Our young family on our arrival to Australia.
My Father and Mother and older brother Danny.*

A younger version of me.

My primary school days.

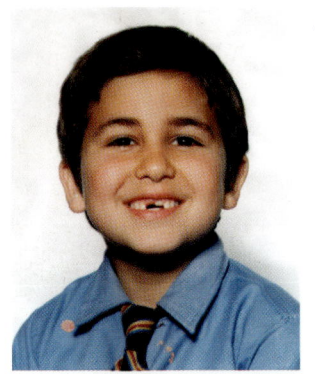

*My Under 16s team the Parramatta Wildcats.
Back row second from left: a young Justin Harrison
who went on to play Rugby for the Australian Wallabies.
I'm the first one on the left side of the bottom row.*

*My 21st birthday, my brother Danny and my close friend
Leon Trimmingham who had a very big impact on my life.*

One of my false starts.
My short stint playing professional basketball overseas.

My team, Rosaire Basketball club. An experience I won't forget.

In Paris during my life-changing journey.

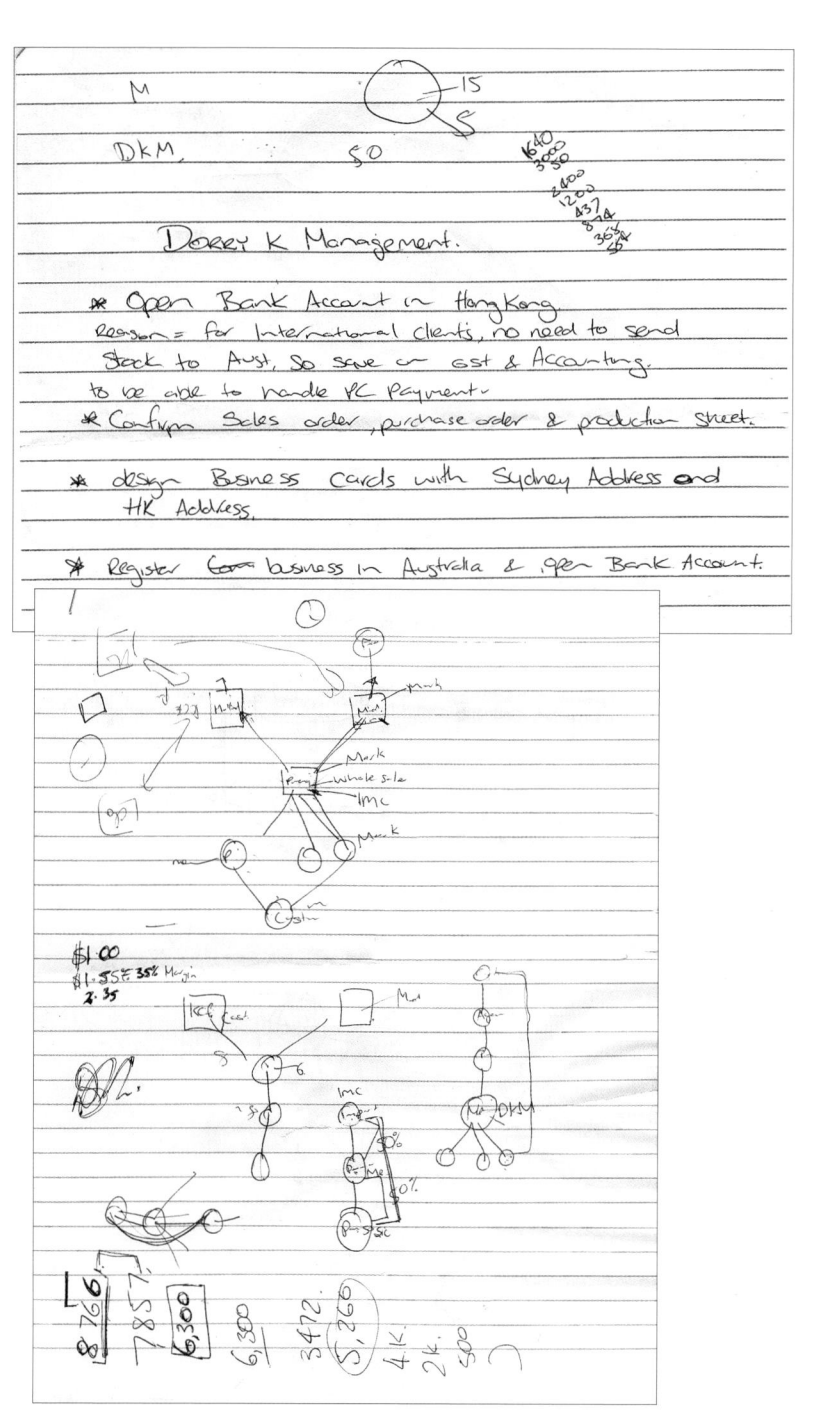

My business plan that I worked on while I was away on my 6-month European journey.

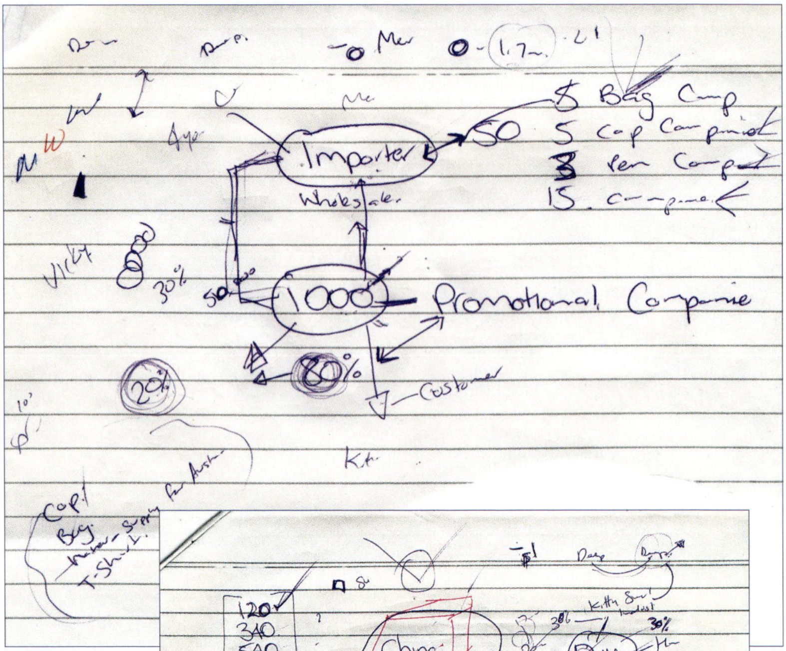
Importer
Wholesaler
50
5 Bag Comp
15
1000
Promotional Companie
80%
20%
30%
Customer
Cap
Bag
T-Shirt

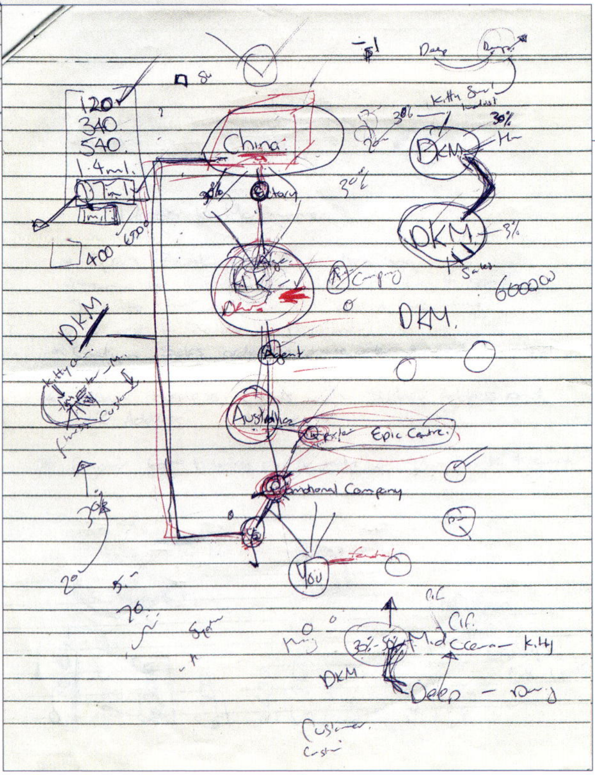
120
340
540
1.4 ml
China
30%
HK
Agent
Australia
Epic Centre
Promotional Company
You
DKM
3%
6000w
Deep
Customer

The next big move, building DKM's first headquarters in Leichhardt.

One of the many moments in which I live on my phone.

- Use realistic expectations to gauge your success.
- Listen to critics but never let them convince you that you are less than you are. Question their motivation. Some critics will tear you down to make themselves look bigger and better, while others will offer critical advice to help you improve yourself.
- Give your time and energy to others. It generates positive feedback and respect. These are the building blocks for self-respect, which are essential to believing in one's self.

Believe in yourself and you will achieve your best. Don't let people knock you down. If someone says you can't do something, don't accept it without question. Don't dismiss it either. Analyse why they say something won't work.

Learn from other people's mistakes

In my experience, common sense is, more often than not, uncommon. The general idea is that we must learn from our own mistakes. I say there is no reason that we cannot learn from other people's mistakes instead! The internet, books, magazines and business networks are filled with case studies for the small business owner to learn from so they do not have to make the same mistakes before understanding a concept or how a strategy will or will not work.

Analyse how in order to avoid incorporating the same failed elements into your business. Here are some examples of famous mistakes made by some very prominent businesses. Apply the lessons from these examples to your business and leverage their blunders into your success.

Case Study 1
When Bill Gates launched Windows 98, his presentation in front of a live CNN audience was marred by what was later referred to as the 'blue screen of death'. The Lesson: A little preparation goes a long way. You cannot afford to give users negative experiences with a new product/service.

Case Study 2
New Coke was the unofficial moniker of a sweeter formulation introduced in 1985 by The Coca-Cola Company to replace its flagship drink, Coca-Cola (Coke). New Coke was a flop, forcing The Coca-Cola Company to revert back to its original Coke formula. The Lesson: If you have spent time developing your brand or have a popular product or service, be sure of your improvements. The Coca-Cola Company came out with New Coke in an attempt to rejuvenate stagnating sales, erroneously thinking that, since sales were down, the popularity of their flagship product must be waning. Many times, slumping sales may be the result of other strategic or operational holes in your business, not necessarily the product itself. Coke failed to consider this before attempting to reinvent the wheel.

Case Study 3

An event that handed Starbucks the first place prize in CNN Money's Dumbest Marketing Moves of the Year was an email campaign that quickly went awry. Several stores were encouraged to send an email to friends and family members with a coupon for a free drink. I don't know about you but I still get emails telling me that, if I forward the email to others, Bill Gates will send me $100. In no time at all, Starbucks had thousands of free drink coupons floating around with no way to contain or track them. The Lesson: Before you roll out an incentive, coupon, free offer, etc., make sure you know what your maximum spend will be and how far that incentive can go. Set parameters around the special offer programs and think through the distribution model so you understand and manage your reach.

These are just a few examples of the hundreds of learning opportunities big businesses present small business owners every day. By constructively studying everything that isn't working in the world of business and relating it back to your business, you can eliminate many of the costly mistakes your business might otherwise make. Thank the Microsofts, Starbucks and Coca Colas of the world for making your business choices easier and saving you money!

Notes

Chapter Four

Discovering My Purpose

If your eyes are open and your spirit is willing, opportunities in life can come from anywhere, even the most unlikely sources. Train yourself to be consciously aware of everything that is happening around you — every word that is spoken, every action that occurs and every encounter you experience. Something as innocuous as overhearing a conversation about how a widget could be that much better if only it offered an XYZ component, can generate in you an inspired thought — an idea that might easily become the next Liquid Paper or Post-It Note. Think of just how simple those inventions really are and the money they made their inventors, after they hit the market. It might not be an actual invention; it could be an idea that fills a niche for a service not currently provided. It might be that you learn of a business that would benefit from someone with your particular skill set.

Ideas come to us at the strangest times. Ever find yourself looking at a sunset when suddenly a little voice inside you says, "Hey, what about trying your hand at...?"

If you never listen, if you never try, you'll never know. If your mind is closed to that little voice, if your eyes are blinkered to what is happening around you, if your ears are not attuned to listen to what people are saying, a myriad of opportunities are passing you by, unnoticed.

When I was 16 years old, I began working for my cousin, George, in the shoe department of his sports store. I discovered I was a natural at sales because I love talking with people. George later moved on to start up a business he named ICM, selling t-shirts and polo shirts wholesale. Later, my older brother, Danny, joined him. By this time, I was working for my father in the hairdressing business. When I turned 21, George took me aside and said, "Listen, I'd like you to work with me in sales. Will you think about it?" I did think about it. I thought, yes, I'd like to be someone who wears a suit to work every day. I'd like to feel like a real businessperson, someone who goes out to negotiate deals and hold meetings. I've always desired that. My dad didn't want to lose me, so, I decided I'd work for George Monday to Friday and continue working for my father on weekends. This gave me the chance to dip my toe in the world of sales without relinquishing my hold on my existing career.

From the very first day, I felt a rivulet of excitement. I knew sales was where my future lay, a field where I could make a successful career for myself. "I will do this for a very long time," I said to myself. "This is going to give me what I need to achieve my dreams." And it has.

Chapter Four | **Discovering My Purpose**

After all this time, I am still in sales and still loving it. I have progressed, I have made a lot of money and I have created a lot of opportunities, but it was more than that. I felt in my gut that sales was my calling, that this was going to be my break. All because I was open to what was going on around me, because I listened to that little voice. No earth-shattering occurrence out of my control dramatically spun my life in a different direction. Someone simply pointed out a new path and I thought, why not? I made the choice to take those first few steps.

George's business at that stage was focused on wholesaling polo and t-shirts. The products were purchased plain to sell to companies who then would print them up with their own designs and sell them to their own corporate clients. When I first began working there, I was thrown into the deep end. I knew next to nothing about garments or weight or fabric, let alone industry terminology. One of my first meetings was with a potential customer who brought along one of his sales people. My brother told me to just, "make it up as you go along, if you have to". He threw me a 180-gram t-shirt and said, "Go sell it". I walked into the meeting and bluffed my way through as best I could. Even though the client had easily 15 years of industry experience, he left with the impression that I knew my stuff — even though I didn't. He even commented on the fact that I seemed to know a fair bit about the product although I was fairly young. I claimed that I'd just learned as I went along.

At the age of 21, I had found my niche, in the sales arena and I was immediately convinced of my abilities. Eventually, Dad accepted that I wouldn't be taking over his business and, thankfully, he didn't try to force the issue. He did, however, implore my cousin to convince me that I would do better running my own business than I would selling for someone else. I like to think that my father enjoyed a wry smile when, three years later, I left my cousin's business to play professional basketball in Lebanon. Likely he may have even felt a sense of relief, as my brother and I both working for our cousin had led to some tense moments of sibling rivalry.

Looking back, I remember the fights my brother and I had as if they were yesterday. I wasn't willing to listen and Danny wasn't willing to let me run off like a loose cannon adopting my own philosophies, so of course, we clashed. Danny was already working in the company when I started and while most of the fights arose because he was older than me and wanted me to do exactly as he said, the fact was I excelled in sales without taking his advice. Eighteen months down the track, George's sister, Lina, wanted to start up a merchandise business. George asked me to help her. I was more than a bit disappointed and even nervous about going into a start-up company. I felt I'd earned the right to stay with George and Danny but they were merging their business with two other companies. They both knew it would give an extremely bad impression to their new partners if they witnessed

Chapter Four | Discovering My Purpose

the Kordahi brothers constantly at each other's throats. In essence, I was fired and I felt sick about it. I knew I was lucky to have been offered an alternative but I was upset and angry at being pushed out. Having said that, part of me was secretly pleased because with the new business would be new challenges and I do like to test myself, even if it did mean moving out of comfortable surroundings.

Lina had formed her new company, Deep, from her bedroom in Clovelly, with no clients. I was 23. I was given every cold caller's bible — the Yellow Pages. Lina told me there was a wealth of clients in that book and to pick a section, start calling and try to sell our services. It was a tough ask as I had to sell our business with little to offer. It was nerve-racking and I was rejected repeatedly.

I decided to approach all the gyms, as I felt comfortable with my sporting background. After countless attempts, I began to make some progress and manoeuvred to set meetings with small gyms that were content only to place small orders, no more than 50 t-shirts. To me, any size order was a positive.

One day I took a deep breath and telephoned the Australia Institute of Sport (AIS) and talked my way up to the head buyer. I built a rapport with him over the phone in a short time. The quantities he was considering were huge, several thousand t-shirts, bags, caps and various other products. I was so excited. I was convinced I had struck it big. This would be the biggest sale in my sales career so far. After numerous discussions, the head buyer scheduled a trip to Sydney to discuss his requirements further. I was nervous and spent a lot of time ensuring that the room in Lina's house was set for the next day's meeting. I couldn't sleep a wink that night.

The following day, I arrived at Lina's early, anxious that all would be perfect for the two o'clock meeting. I waited and waited. Two o'clock came and went, with no sign of the client. Attempts to reach him by phone were unsuccessful. I was baffled and deeply disappointed. I racked my brain, trying to figure out what I'd done wrong, what could have happened. As I looked around, the realisation hit me. He had no doubt arrived at the house, realised this was a home-based business and decided there was no way a prominent outfit like the AIS was going to place such a huge order with some fly-by-night outfit. Looking back now I can laugh but at the time it left me feeling profoundly disheartened. I knew I had to go on and focus on smaller clients who wouldn't baulk at our location.

My memories of this period are mainly of tough times. I felt rudderless. I had lost direction and lost touch with something I really loved to do. I had no understanding of the merchandising industry. I'd gone from a comfortable corporate office to a room in a house in the suburbs, which I found demotivating. I recall my parents' deep concern, watching as I worked as hard as I could and barely earning a cent. I worked for a year without income to help the business, drawing unemployment benefits to pay the bills. I was driving a beat-up old van; I had absolutely nothing. I'd rustle up $100 here and there, to help me survive but it was intensely frustrating to be unable to afford to buy so much as a drink if I went out with friends. I would order water or a beer to hold in my hand for hours so as not to feel conspicuous while mixing with the crowd.

Many of my friends advised me I was wasting my time. Why not get a proper job and earn an income, they asked. Part of me agreed with the sentiment but another part told me to learn what I could, to identify what other possibilities existed in the world. I told my well-meaning critics to wait and see where I will be in five years time and then we could decide if I was truly wasting my time. I was determined to maintain a positive attitude, a belief in myself and in my never-say-die passion to succeed.

I had many false starts before my star began to shine. There were many bumps and bruises on my road to success but through it all, yes, I stood tall and did it my way, never losing my drive and never losing my self-belief. Success speaks for itself. I had had enough of the negative comments ridiculing me and what my intentions were. Nothing or no one, I decided, was going to stop me from doing exactly what I had planned. These thoughts were a catalyst, fuelling my drive even more. But in the interim, despite this belief, I found I couldn't ignore the call of the wild, or, in my case, the call to return to Lebanon. (At this point, I should mention that I had already been to Lebanon twice before, both times touring with the Australian Lebanese basketball team. While I was there, one of the local team scouts had apparently spotted me.)

A fax arrived from the president of the Rosaire Basketball Club asking to speak with me. I telephoned him and was stunned to learn he wanted me to try out for their team.

My cousin's fledgling business didn't have many clients, so I decided she could manage well enough without me. I wanted to explore this once-in-a-lifetime opportunity to become a professional basketball player in the Middle East. Perhaps there was a tinge of opportunism but when Fate was dealing me such a card, I felt it would be foolhardy to ignore it only to spend the rest of my days wondering, "what if?"

Two days later, I was on a flight bound for Lebanon.

After a short trial with the team, they liked what they saw and offered me a player contract. After two more weeks, I flew back to Australia to organise a few final details and returned to Lebanon two months later. My parents were thrilled. Needless to say, it was the most exciting adventure I had ever had. I was ecstatic to have the chance to be the best I could be at my chosen sport and to play overseas. It is every person's dream to do what they love and be paid for it!

I arrived in Beirut in time for the pre-season camp. Playing in a foreign country was a real challenge.

Chapter Four | **Discovering My Purpose**

Admittedly, Lebanon was my place of birth, but I had lived all my life in Australia. Still, I was energised by the connection I felt.

Our training schedule was three times a day, six days a week. I lost the sense of passing time. I had days that felt like that movie, Groundhog Day. Day in, day out, our coach pushed us to our limits.

Whatever path you follow, whether it is sport, business, or anything else, it comes with its own unique set of challenges. Mental strength, along with emotional intelligence, plays a major part in how far you are prepared to go to be the best you can be.

Playing professionally overseas did come with its perks. I soon found myself on the front cover of sports magazines, on TV and being recognised for my profession. It was exhilarating. Amongst all the hype, it could have been easy to get derailed and lose focus on my goal.

Our first pre-season game took place in a small village against Sagesse, the Lebanese and Asian champions. I played for more than 30 minutes. I was guarding Elie Mchantaf who, at that time, was the best player in Lebanon. It was pretty daunting but I managed to keep his scoring to a reasonable number.

A few months into my contract I began feeling the strain of internal club politics. The president had his favourite player, another point guard and issues arose concerning me getting more court time than the other player did. The situation became so bad that I requested they release me so I could play with another team. I was frustrated. To make matters worse, they wouldn't release me until it suited them. The cut-off date for transfers was August 30th. To my disgust, they waited until August 31 to release me, to prevent me from playing with any other team. It was difficult not to feel bitter but, at age 23, I felt I had to accept that it just wasn't meant to be.

Deciding my goals and aspirations lay in the realm of the business world after all, I turned my back on professional basketball for what I thought would be the final time. The umbilical cord had been severed this time forever, I told myself. Nothing could have been farther from the truth.

In the meantime, I flew back to Australia and focused on Lina's business, by which time George and Danny had become involved. The combined business interests were getting traction and attracting more and more clients to the point where relocation to bigger premises became imperative. A more well-defined structure emerged and I found myself feeling comfortable in the corporate environment, enjoying a new sense of security and stability.

The business soon expanded and we secured several substantial accounts which yielded consistent cash flow to where we could afford to hire the additional staff we needed. The company continued to expand and soon we found ourselves relocating yet again, to even bigger premises. My confidence was also growing as my understanding of the industry increased.

I turned my focus to gaining bigger and bigger clients. At this point I was managing numerous clients, each turning over just a few thousand dollars at a time. I looked at my production reports. I would have 80 jobs in production, with a total value of roughly $90,000. I needed to work smarter, I thought, not harder. I targeted the clients who had what I felt was the greatest potential and focused on them. This approach is referred to as the Pareto principle, or 80-20 rule, where roughly 80 percent of the yield comes from 20 percent of the sources. In my case, this meant focusing on the 20 percent of clients that offered the greatest dollar value return.

The following year I turned over $1.2 million in sales with considerably less effort. Despite the numbers, I was still the youngest of the four and knew I was last in everyone's minds. I felt somehow that I was going backwards instead of forwards. I had generated $1.2 million in sales but wasn't being given a chance to develop. The look in their eyes said, "We are more experienced and we know more, so let us handle things". I, instead, was impatient, wanting to test my ability and push my boundaries.

It didn't help that I thought I was underpaid. Friends in the industry were being paid $60,000 to $80,000 for turning over $800,000 in sales. I, on the other hand, was turning over more than a million dollars in sales and getting $55,000 a year for my efforts. The disputes over salary were constant. I wanted to do right by the family but at the time they wanted to hire and pay $45,000 apiece to two people to turn over $500,000 each in sales. I said, "Wait a minute. Do the math. I'm turning over more than a million dollars in sales and you want to pay these people $90,000 combined to do the same? Why shouldn't I be getting $90,000 then?" It seemed logical to me. This didn't go down well with George and Lina, however. Still, I was convinced I was right and was determined to stand up for myself.

For me I saw business in an incisive way: the need to keep it simple and effective. As I looked around, I spotted warning signs. For example, we spent money continually on infrastructure rather than making money for the business. Even though the business was turning over a lot of money, it wasn't holding on to it. This appeared to me to be a poor strategy. In simple terms, if we weren't making sufficient profits, then how could we consider it to be a profitable business? It seemed grossly apparent to me that the business was overcapitalising.

My disappointment grew as my passion for the business shrank. When my chance to become a sales manager was shot down, I knew I'd reached a turning point. I was told I was too young and had no real experience in management. I felt I had no choice. I resigned.

I told Danny I'd show him how to run a business properly. Danny told me it wasn't as easy as I thought and to stop being such a smartass.

Chapter Four | Discovering My Purpose

I still lacked a vision for my first solo enterprise. In my quest for inspiration and direction, I decided on a radical approach. I left Australia.

So began the next phase of my odyssey. It was the toughest, scariest thing I'd ever done yet. I left security behind to step into the unknown. And, let me tell you, that step out of my comfort zone was a giant, terrifying leap. There were dark moments when I was riddled with self-doubt. How could I be so stupid? So foolish? How could I walk out on my family business without knowing where I was going?

I squared my shoulders. If I had the willpower to take that first step, I reasoned, then I had the willpower to achieve something big. I didn't want to be a follower. I wanted to be a leader. I didn't want to be a dreamer. I wanted to be a doer.

I set off on what was intended to be a 10-week fact-finding trip to Europe. Ten weeks turned into six months, as the vision of my future began to materialise.

Although I was enjoying the new experiences and new people like on any vacation, I also knew I was preparing for the next stage in my life to take flight. It was while I was in London that I experienced an epiphany of sorts. And I soon discovered the clarity it brings.

Entrepreneurial Strategies – Chapter Four

- Recognise and reward staff
- Don't blur the lines between business and friendship
- Tips for starting out

Recognise and reward staff
Good staff is invaluable. If you want to hold on to your staff and build a strong, loyal culture within your business, consider implementing a reward scheme. The key to good management is to identify what drives your employees individually. Discover the stimulus that pushes them to strive for greatness. The reward need not be monetary. It could be a bonus day off to spend with their family or even an extra hour for lunch.

A points programme where employees who achieve delineated goals earn points towards a free dinner or a vacation is another possibility. One caveat: If you bribe your staff, there's a risk they will come to expect it as part of their normal compensation. I prefer to reward my people on a merit basis as it's often more appreciated.

If you thank a manufacturing group every time they make customer deliveries on time by providing them with a free lunch, gradually the lunch becomes a given, an entitlement and is no longer viewed as a reward. For example, in one organisation, the CEO traditionally bought lunch for all employees every Friday. Soon, he had employees asking to be reimbursed if they ate lunch outside of the company on Fridays. His goal of team building turned into an entitlement, with disappointing results.

Employee recognition is not just about doing something nice for people. Employee recognition is a communication tool that reinforces and rewards the most important outcomes people create for your business. When you recognise people effectively, you reinforce with your chosen means of recognition the actions and behaviours you most want to promote. When considering an employee recognition process, bear in mind you must develop recognition that is equally powerful for both the organisation and the employee.

Figuring out the most effective methods to reward and recognise employees is no simple task. The key thing is to express appreciation. A small thank you or acknowledgment has a positive impact.

Take the time to acknowledge and personally thank those employees who have improved production, efficiency and the overall mood of the office or job site.

Don't blur the lines between business and friendship
Finding the right balance boils down to respect. Oftentimes when small businesses start up, they naturally involve family and friends. After all, it is family and friends who support you through thick and thin and want you to succeed. But balancing the needs

between personal and business relationships can be tricky if respect is not present. That means not giving — or expecting — special treatment when a personal relationship exists. This is equally important for those co-workers with whom you do not have a special relationship. It's imperative to treat everyone the same in business, no matter what the connection.

Set a tone of professional respect. All too often, managers confuse building camaraderie among employees with creating an overly familiar environment. When the work environment becomes too familiar, it is easy for employees to feel comfortable sniping and griping. And this is something you want to avoid at all costs!

Leadership involves motivating the entire staff to share a common vision. You can't effectively lead if you're trying to cultivate personal relationships instead of professional ones. If snipes and gripes begin to permeate your office culture, you must stop being a buddy and start being a leader. Direct your staff towards productive problem-solving sessions and activities to create the momentum to move forward.

Camaraderie, social activities, trust and sincerity are all important traits in a leader, but it is important to draw the line at becoming a friend to every team member. Being a leader is a very different role than being a friend or relative. You cannot be an objective leader, one who carries out the tough decisions and provides the necessary coaching/performance feedback to employees if you are also trying to be their friend or tiptoe around the implied debt of a family connection. Plenty of friend and family relationships have been damaged this way. Instead, cultivate a strong environment of trust and insist everyone keep things professional.

Tips for starting out

When I left the family business, I was wary of the unknown. My business grew quickly, but here are some tips that might have made that fear-filled stage easier.

Tip 1

Map out a strategy. Make a to-do list, crunch the numbers and marshal your human and production resources. It is always easier to fight a battle in your head or on paper or computer spreadsheet than to shoot first and ask questions later. No matter how much pressure you're getting from your customers to deliver the goods right now, you need to take the time to sit down and map out a plan of attack. For a manufacturing company or a wholesale distributor, this means estimating how many units of product your customers might buy and how much it would cost to produce or import them. A service company like an ad agency or a web design firm must estimate how many additional employees or independent contractors are necessary to service the expected influx of new accounts.

If your company already has employees, ask if they're willing to put in a few extra hours to help you get over the hump. If you're a one person show, reach out to friends and family members to give you a temporary hand or, if they lack the necessary skills, post ads on websites to find skilled freelancers and independent contractors. Be aware that your overnight success may not last forever. Don't commit to hiring full-time employees with payroll taxes and benefits until you're sure your company's good fortune is secure.

Tip 2

Forge production partnerships. A small business making handcrafted soaps is going to be hard-pressed to fill a million-unit order from a large national chain all by itself. Partner with manufacturers who can take your samples or prototypes and reproduce them in large quantities. While there's no shortage of suppliers listed on the internet, a reliable manufacturer that delivers high-quality goods is not so easy to find. Your best bet may be to contact your industry's trade association and its leading trade publications (industry newspapers) for consultants and referrals.

Tip 3

Communicate with your customers. Communication is the lifeblood of any business relationship but it is even more critical when your product or service suddenly takes off. The biggest mistake a business owner can make is failing to warn customers of shipping or production delays until it is too late.

Companies who fail to communicate with their key customers may find themselves not only with egg on their faces but with unsold inventory in their warehouses as well. There are so many things that are beyond your control. I would rather tell my customers the truth and have them be angry at me for five minutes than make excuses and burn my bridges forever.

Tip 4
Invest for the future. While it's tempting to reap the profits from your hit product right away, it is important to reinvest some of those profits to help your business grow. Whether this translates to paying down debt, buying new equipment, hiring employees or opening another location, don't pass up this opportunity to make your money work for you. It is always cheaper to put your own cash to work for you than to borrow money from a bank or relinquish equity to an investor.

Notes

Chapter Five

Turning the Vision into Reality

I have always loved dealing, trading and negotiating. It has always been a part of who I am. When I was selling shoes, even at that young age, I would instinctively try to up-sell clients to two pairs of shoes instead of one, or guide the clients into a more expensive, better quality product.

The gift of the gab and an ability to relate to people helps a lot here. I've always been a good talker and I have always loved helping people. So for me it was natural. I never went to university, never completed a TAFE course or obtained a marketing degree. It has all been about putting myself in the buyer's shoes, so to speak and listening to and perceiving what it is they want.

Empathy is as important as vision and just about as hard to teach. There is little doubt, however, that any successful businessperson possesses the ability to read the person sitting on the opposite side of the table. And not just to read them, but to visualise five steps ahead, like a chess player, instead of only one.

When I left Australia, I travelled throughout Europe, staying with anyone I knew to keep down costs. One of them was my other cousin, George, in Paris. He was heading southeast to Saint-Tropez for a holiday and suggested I accompany him. I knew nothing of Saint-Tropez, least of all that it was a playground for the rich and famous.

My cousin had hired a villa for a month at Sainte-Maxime, a nearby bay. From the moment I arrived, my eyes lit up and I was overwhelmed by the lifestyle and the magnitude of the wealth I saw about me.

For ten days it was non-stop partying at nightclubs until four or five o'clock in the morning, heading back to the villa for a quick nap, only to start all over again.

The first night I went to the V.I.P Room, reputed to be one of the best clubs. While there, I saw a sign for a Bad Boy party the following night, Bad Boy being the famous rapper, P. Diddy. It turned out to be a red carpet, invitation only event. Celebrities were waltzing in, the paparazzi were out in force and everyone was dressed to the nines. I watched as a car pulled up and P. Diddy emerged.

I thought, "How the hell am I going to get in to this party?" It took me half an hour to pluck up my courage but I figured, "What the heck, I'm in another country, nobody here knows me."

My cousin was back at the villa and so if I got tossed out no one would find out. Taking a deep breath, I walked towards the entrance. There were 15 or so people ahead of me. To my amazement the bouncer looked me up and down, parted the crowd and waved me through. I don't know who on earth he mistook me for but I got in.

Inside, guests were outdoing each other, buying the most expensive Champagnes. Meanwhile, I stood holding my solitary beer which had cost a shocking price, taking tiny sips and trying to make it last all night. I saw a world I had never seen before or even realised existed. If anything, this made me even hungrier for the extreme success I knew could be mine if I strove hard enough.

The next day I linked up with the same glitterati on Nikki Beach where the festivities continued. With strains of "if my friends could see me now", strumming through my brain, I returned to the V.I.P Room. Twenty metres from the entrance, the bouncer spotted me. By the time I had reached the door, he had parted the crowd to permit me to pass. To this day, I suspect he had confused me with someone else but back then I wasn't about to ask. What I did discover was that wealth and success brought privilege and status and I wanted it — more than ever!

After finagling my way into other purportedly impenetrable VIP nightspots across Europe, I started to ask myself some penetrating questions. If I were to start a company and sell products from the modest back garden of my parent's home, how would I convince people to buy from me? Would I need to lower my margins and undercut all the competition? Or should I make my company look like a million dollars and focus on branding and brand placement? With my new penchant for the finer things, quality and luxury, I chose the latter. This wasn't solely based on a purely hedonistic attitude but rather on the observation that most of my prospective competitors in the marketplace were just going through the motions of moving product.

My perspective was shaped by my European experience, where I witnessed firsthand the significant differences between the promotions industry in Australia versus overseas. Europe is very image conscious. Everything is so well done. They have so much style. You don't see the usual gear; everything is carefully thought out. I began to wonder why Australians didn't take the same degree of care with their image as Europeans did with theirs.

In Australia, armed with a bag of goodies and a catalogue, the competition almost exclusively relied on customers to sell to themselves. If I was to make my company look like a million dollars, I needed to differentiate myself from the competition. I didn't need a degree to open up a promotional business but I knew I would need a philosophy of branding, brand platforms, high quality work and, equally as important, the ability to manage clients' needs and expectations instead of just telling them what they should need. In other words, I was going to turn the traditional promotional methods upside down. I would position myself as an assistant to my clients, an indispensable right arm they could trust and rely upon without question. After all, the more a person trusts, the less they question. In other words, the more they feel comfortable with how you do business, the less likely the client is to shop around for alternatives. This has been my philosophy from day one, and it works.

My business has continued to grow and improve because I view it from a management perspective, not a product perspective. To me, the product is secondary. Sure, I can put a logo onto a cap or print it onto a t-shirt, but what sets my firm apart is how we approach making the client's job easier, saving them time which, in turn, increases their reliance upon us. The smart clients are not going to give their business away to someone else to save 10 cents if they are spending 30 percent more time to save that 10 cents.

I began with the vision that the merchandising industry should be mainly about managing clients' expectations. I didn't want to be a provider of merchandise. I looked at it from the perspective that I would manage their business by becoming part of their marketing team. If they didn't have a marketing team, well, then I was going to be their marketing manager, marketing assistant or brand manager. With that strategy, I would elevate my business beyond needing to compete with my so-called competitors. I created a niche market where, instead of competing on price, I competed on concepts and ideas. It took me six months to plan my strategy, which gave me both the time and the materials to surmount any fears of failure I experienced.

I spent many days in London walking the streets for hours and hours, assessing all the positives and negatives. I spent months visualising the potholes in business and how I would overcome them. I changed my return flight six times, determined not to return until I was as fully prepared as possible and had a clear direction of the way I was going to build my business — my empire. I had no intention of starting my own business until those thoughts were straight in my mind. Once I had it all worked out, I flew home the very next day and began.

When I returned from Europe, my family probably thought I'd walk in with my tail between my legs, begging to return to the family business. It would not have been unreasonable to assume that a holiday would calm my state of mind. But I came back fired up, ready to challenge myself, affirming to myself that there was no room whatsoever for failure. I certainly didn't intend to return to cutting people's hair for the rest of my life and I had even less intention of crawling back to my cousin's business. Somewhere, somehow, I was determined to find the answers, to make it on my own.

I hate losing. I'm extremely competitive. I'm a fighter and whether it may be called pride or determination, nothing was going to beat me down. Taking that first step into the unknown is probably one of the hardest steps any person will ever take but taking it is what sets you apart, as someone who takes action, not someone who is going to hold back because of either fear or disbelief — or both. I knew I wasn't going to return to Australia until everything was clear in my head.

I am asked sometimes about what difficult times I've had in business and I can't really say I've had too many. I think this is due to my mental approach prior to setting up the business of working through all the potential potholes before I'd even started.

I committed to constantly pushing myself beyond the boundaries of my own comfort zone. Having already faced the biggest challenge of leaving the family business to go it alone in the wilderness, without any kind of formal education behind me, I knew I had no room for failure. That was not a place I was prepared to go. All I had to start this empire was a desk, a computer and a whole heap of attitude. I built a website, printed up some business cards and the adventure began. I managed all aspects of the business. I was the sales manager, the accountant, the production manager and the logistics manager. I made sure I knew every part of my business before I contemplated hiring anyone. It was important to me to gain experience in all aspects of my business and doing so allowed me to understand the roles my future staff members would play. I kept it simple and used spreadsheets for invoicing. I created a numeric tracking system for my orders. My parents' backyard became a shipyard. I would receive stock from China and have to hold over 100 boxes at a time. It was like a makeshift external warehouse where I would run my logistics by doing the labelling and despatching myself. Back then my entire marketing pack was printed on a single piece of A4 paper.

When I first started, a lot of suppliers failed to support me the way I needed because they saw me as a small-time, backyard operator. The few who did support me are among those I use today. I have been loyal to those who have helped me build my business, in appreciation for their loyalty. We continue to grow our commercial relationship and for that I am very thankful. The positive side of this relationship is that it affords me negotiating power with my suppliers, allowing me to remain competitive in the market. The lesson learnt here is that building a strong supplier relationship is a critical part of one's business. They have seen my business grow to the success it is today and they have been rewarded with gaining my business. Today we have a lot of suppliers knocking on our door wanting to offer their services. I stay true to those who looked after me when I ran my logistics from the backyard of my parents' home.

Keep in mind that, before you start placing orders overseas, you must calculate how much working capital you will need to meet the market demand. Because employees and manufacturers generally won't wait until you've sold the products and collected the money before you pay them, you'll need a source of capital that you can tap into immediately.

One hurdle I faced was being respected as a business leader. I always had a bit of a complex about being seen as too young. I feared people wouldn't take me seriously when it came to business. I had experienced this as part of the family business and didn't want the same thing to happen within my own business. When I started DKM eight years ago at the age of 26, I was driven to succeed and to show everyone not to judge me by my age but by my success and work ethic. Maybe I worried too much about it as, for a short time, I was filled with a lot of self-doubt. However, in hindsight, it also served to give me the desire to work harder than the next person and push myself to heights I never previously thought I could achieve. Pretty soon I stopped worrying about the age factor.

Just as Richard Branson had done, I created the impression to the outside world that I was running a sizeable and established business, when, in fact I was working from inside a garden shed. Even if a prospective customer hadn't heard of me, I managed to convince them to give me a try and, if I couldn't deliver, then I didn't expect them to buy from me. So, as a fledging entrepreneur, I was ready to test my wings and to see if they would allow me to soar to great heights or plummet to my doom before I could figure out how to make them flap.

The moment I returned from Europe, I headed straight to register DKM (Dorry Kordahi Management) as a company and from that point I have never looked back. Within six months, this fledgling entrepreneur had taken his first faltering flight into the world of the business tycoon. I was acquiring a sound client base with my unique approach to branding and making a profit almost from Day One.

I even inspired my older brother, Danny. Upon seeing how quickly I was establishing myself, he thought, "If he can do it, so can I!" So Danny then left the family business and went and registered his own company under the name DK Blue.

All too soon it was time to think about hiring my first employee. First, I elicited some assistance from my good friend, Elisa Grant, whom I first met at an industry event, the Australian Promotional Products Association's (APPA) Christmas function back when I was still working for Lina, my cousin. Elisa and I became friends and she spent a lot of time with me, brainstorming ways in which I could succeed in my own business.

Working only a suburb away from each other, I would meet Elisa for lunch regularly. We would bounce ideas off one another and talk about the industry, exploring ways in which we could maximise our business opportunities. She also furnished me with leads when she knew she couldn't satisfy the client through her organisation.

Now that I needed to hire someone, I knew Elisa could help. Elisa had been a recruitment consultant prior to coming into the industry, so we had very different backgrounds. Hers was strong in direct sales because, in recruitment, you are essentially selling thin air; it is quite different from selling tangible products. She'd also been to university and completed several sales courses. As a result of our numerous conversations, I began to view certain aspects of my planning in a different light. This experience was very beneficial. It was a strong complement of skills, education and experience that we brought to the table. We would endlessly discuss suppliers and supply channels and I would quiz her on how a person could sell if they didn't really know what they were selling (i.e. recruitment). She explained how it didn't really matter what you were selling, that sales principles are consistent no matter what the product or service.

Even though she'd only been in the brand merchandising business about six months when we met, she had already won some significant accounts. I knew I could sell but I was hungry to learn how she achieved her results and, in return, I offered her the benefit of my years of industry knowledge.

I discussed my need to hire someone with Elisa. It took about six months before it actually came to fruition and by that time she had begun working for Corporate Express.

Her new company was one of the major players in our industry. I remember her asking me how I imagined I could compete with such a giant organisation and I replied, "Believe me, I'll compete!" My reasoning was that, the bigger you are, the harder it is to manoeuvre. I explained I'd rather be a swift cheetah, able to dart in a different direction with deft ease when chasing its prey, than a lumbering elephant that had only its size to rely on.

She laughed, but during that six-month period when she came to my office in the back garden, I continued to pepper her with questions and get her to help without ever actually employing her.

The first employee I hired was my younger brother, David. At the time, David was working in retail for many years with no clear direction. He came to me and asked if I could give him an opportunity in a new field. I insisted he be formally interviewed before I made my decision. I asked Elisa if she would assist with the interviewing process. She was surprised but my reasoning was sound. I had already learned from having operated within a family business that sharing the same blood does not equate to working well together. Elisa was experienced both in my chosen industry and in recruitment, so even though I might be putting her in a bit of a spot, I knew she would make an unbiased and informed assessment as to whether or not I should hire David.

Elisa suggested we conduct the interview in a local pub. Although the atmosphere was relaxed and casual, the conversation was extremely serious and pointed. After the interview concluded, Elisa and David shared

Chapter Five | Turning the Vision into Reality

a few glasses of wine and a laugh. At this time, Elisa advised David that this was in fact a serious business he would be joining, that it was going places and how his brother wasn't going to employ him simply because he was family. He was going to have to earn his position like any other candidate.

As it turned out, our first attempt at working together may not have felt like a match made in heaven but now our working relationship is a solid one.

Back in the days of working in the garden shed, part of the problem arose with mindset. It might have looked like a garden shed, smelled like a garden shed and been situated in a position where one might expect to find a garden shed, but, to me, this was my first official premises and I expected it to be treated as such. I would dress professionally to go to work. I would go out for my lunch. In every aspect, I treated this garden shed like my corporate office. David, on the other hand, treated it like a garden shed. He wore whatever he felt like and took a nap inside at lunchtime. Annoyed, I asked him if he'd do that in an office. Of course not, he said, but this wasn't an office, he pointed out. It was a garden shed. And therein lay the difference in attitude between us. It required a mental willingness, a discipline to treat the business as a business, no matter what the physical location was. After several months, with regret, I felt I had no option but to fire David because he stubbornly refused to share the DK philosophy. I suggested he work with our older brother,

Danny, so that he would have to commute to work and understand and appreciate the importance of discipline.

Unrelenting in my pursuit of Elisa to become an employee of DKM, I would frequently speak at length to her about leaving her high-flying, secure, corporate position to risk it all and join my fledgling empire. Finally I wore her down.

The first three months were tough on Elisa. She thumbed through the Yellow Pages making cold calls to businesses, as I had once previously done in my cousin's apartment. She was in conflict with my philosophies, largely because I wasn't doing things the way they had been done at Corporate Express. I was resolute in my beliefs; it was my way or not at all. Elisa came not only to respect my business nous but over time evolved into one of my biggest advocates.

In an uncharacteristic but mercifully brief period of waning confidence, I grew afraid to expand my business. In my first few years of operation, I had turned over one million dollars and suddenly decided this was comfortable. I didn't want to spend what I saw as an extortionate amount on rent. I was turning over a million dollars without an office after all. The bottom line was that I had let fear seep into my consciousness. I had taken that first terrifying step that some never do, going out on my own. Now I was presented with another challenge — taking the next step. Would we remain forever at a million-dollar turnover working

Chapter Five | Turning the Vision into Reality

out of a garden shed? Certainly I could do worse and certainly this limited my exposure to risk. But was it enough or did I want more? That, of course, was a rhetorical question but to move to the next level, to face that risk head on, to continue challenging myself as I'd always told myself I wanted to do, required me to stick my neck out into unfamiliar territory once again. So I prepared myself mentally and pushed myself out of my comfort zone and into what I hoped was a new tomorrow, pushing my boundary of fear to a new level. Ultimately, the next level became my next comfort zone and, hence, to continue expanding, this entire exercise had to be repeated.

I focused on streamlining the business to the point where I could withstand any turbulence. I built up my cash flow to where, if I didn't have another sale for three years I would still be able to support the business with its current overhead. My aim was to have a secure business where I could dictate to the market, not have the market dictate to me. When companies start making money, they often overcapitalise on unnecessary costs because they either think they need it or they want to impress. A business is measured on profit, not on its turnover.

In an industry with over 2,000 competitors, I realised I would need to bring something different to the table to gain market share rapidly enough. I think it is important to elaborate the difficult industry that I am in. I am not in a retail space or an industry that has huge potential to make large amounts of money. Margins are low and competition fierce. A tendency to bring down the market costs on price wars can naturally have an adverse effect on the industry, not only from a price perspective but also from the point of view that products and services might be devalued in the eyes of marketing and brand managers alike. Remember the focus of where I positioned my business? Not just as someone coordinating logos on tangible goods. I was here to create an impact by being the service provider this industry had never experienced before. I managed to make my money in a tough industry, which turned out to be very rewarding and gave me the reassurance that I was running my business in the direction of growth and prosperity, not just survival.

Elisa was my right-hand person for a good part of the developmental stage. I had the major accounts but Elisa did a lot of the administration, such as compiling the job specifications, creating systems and procedures, as well as forms and everything else one needs in order to grow. She confessed there were periods where she felt it was all too much and she wasn't getting what she needed out of the position. She obviously wanted this to work for both of us, though, so she stuck it out. That decision ultimately paid dividends but it wasn't always that way.

For a long time, Elisa received anything but preferential treatment and that was one of the reasons she would get upset. She would ask why I would get angry with her. She didn't understand initially that she needed to be perceived as leading by example. We couldn't afford to let anyone think that she was given *carte blanche* just because we were friends and the same policy applied to my younger brother, David. Often, she had to prove herself more in some instances and that was something that did cause her some angst.

Criticisms are sometimes levelled at me for being a little too self-assured. I find that laughable because, in business, if you can't come across as supremely confident in what you do and who you are, then you are not going to instil confidence in anyone else. It is a necessary quality in this dog-eat-dog world. You need to set yourself head and shoulders above the crowd if you're going to be noticed and indeed if you are going to be taken seriously.

If you wish to emulate my success, you need to portray confidence and success and believe in yourself but at the same time remember who you really are. Do not forget who it was who helped you get there for, as I have said before, no man is an island. There will always be those you will need to recognise, reward and appreciate along the way.

At the same time, never let the lines blur between business and friendship or indeed business and family. Don't allow people to take advantage of you by making you feel guilty or convince you that you owe them something. Maintain sight of who your friends are and how to maintain those friendships. If these are people who genuinely care about you, they will support you on your journey.

Entrepreneurial Strategies – Chapter Five

- Taking risks sets you apart from the crowd
- Portray confidence
- Never give up

Taking risks sets you apart from the crowd
Every entrepreneur takes risks. You're not going to be successful if you don't but it is important to stipulate that these should be calculated risks. Don't gamble.

Every risk I've taken has been a calculated risk. It hasn't been a risk that is going to jeopardise my business. The lesson is this: when you spend, spend wisely and only spend up to a point where you're not exposing yourself.

Taking a big risk is a gamble but to me it is more important to understand how to risk a little in order to gain a lot.

A successful entrepreneur knows the difference between the right and the wrong opportunity. You are always going to have opportunities in life but you need to identify the right ones to pursue. Don't make the mistake of thinking that, if you don't take up an opportunity, you are going to miss out on getting in the game. Opportunities always arise and the smart entrepreneur is the one who chooses the right opportunity. So, know your limitations. If the risk is so steep it can potentially damage your business then that is an opportunity on which you need to forego.

The keys to managing risk are:
- Recognising why you may fear a certain decision or action and assessing if there is any rational justification for it.
- Knowing that many of the risks you avoid today will reappear again in the future.
- Understanding that growth comes with risk, whether you fail or succeed.
- Realising that risk is not about what other people do, think, feel or believe about your actions or decisions.

You have everything to gain when you take a reasonable risk in life, as well as the potential for loss.

Portray confidence

In business and in life, you have to portray confidence. Without confidence, people aren't going to want to do business with you. When you are trying to sell a product, if you don't believe in your product, how are you going to sell it? You've got to convey that belief in your product. I always say to my staff, if you don't enjoy what you're doing, don't do it, because it's going to show. You need to come across as if you know what you're talking about. So, learn everything you need to know as confidence can only go so far if it has no substance.

If you are scared, it will show. Low self-esteem or fearfulness manifests in slouched shoulders, head slumped, arms folded defensively in front, or hands stuffed in pockets. Confidence is demonstrated by walking tall, shoulders held back, head up, eye contact, arms relaxed at the sides. Those trained in martial arts are said to be less likely to be victims of an attack because of their body language. They've been trained to defend themselves and not to take a weak position. They have confidence.

Try this experiment:

The next time you're in a public place, supermarket, the beach, no matter where, walk past people and look them directly in the eye. You might want to smile a little so they don't think you're being aggressive. You'll be amazed at the number of people who will avert their eyes to avoid looking at you. They'll look down or away but not at you. Of course, in some cultures it is considered rude to look people in the eye. Be sensitive to that. But even where it is not frowned upon, you will find it hard to find ten people confident enough to look back at you. By looking directly at them, in some subconscious way you're communicating that you are not afraid; this is an instinct that goes back to our hunter-gatherer origins. Predators learn to recognise other predators as they have eyes that point forward. Think about the carnivores in the animal kingdom versus the herbivores: the carnivores all have eyes that look ahead, while the herbivores' eyes are angled to the side. Human beings typically no longer view direct eye contact as dangerous or threatening because our hunting instincts are largely extinct in the modern world. Still, it requires confidence. Making eye contact has become an important part of interpersonal relationships on almost every level.

Half the battle is in your mind and the one thing you will never lose control of is your free will to determine how you react to any given situation. You can do something about how you portray your confidence to the world, so the only question that remains is, will you?

Never give up

If you have a dream and you believe with a passion that what you're doing is right, you have to keep telling yourself to get up one more time, every time you are knocked down. You must never forget that each time someone tells you that you can't do something, each time someone says what you're doing doesn't have any market value, each time you hear this negative you have proceeded one step further along the path to finding the person that will say "yes". They're out there; whether they are your first client, your first publisher, your first business partner or whoever else it may be. Keep searching and you will find them.

Notes

Chapter Six

The Fledgling

My business expanded to the point where I was in a position to start looking for my first official premises. My first office was in Stanmore and cost $35,000 a year in rental, which was a little daunting after not having paid any rent previously. I was a bit apprehensive about making such a big financial commitment at the time but it had to be done; it was all part of the plan and all part of the necessary requirements for growth and expansion. Before long, I also took over the office next door, doubling my floor space and remained there for the next five years. At that point in my journey, the company consisted of me, Elisa and three other staff members. One of the next lessons I learned along the way came during this phase — patience.

Managing staff wasn't an issue; however trying to instil my philosophies into new staff members was another matter entirely, especially when dealing with a group of people whose beliefs and drives were at differing levels. In the early stages, I couldn't understand why everyone just didn't see things the way I did. For me it was so obvious it should have been natural. Nonetheless, as I've pointed out before, if everyone thought the same way and achieved at the same level there would be no room in this world for achievers to rise above, to the top. While this may be a self-evident fact, I was not the most patient man in the world; in fact, I was completely the opposite. When I wanted something, I wanted it right then. There were only two time frames in my world — now and never!

When you run a business you need to learn patience and to be calm because not every staff member will possess the same degree of drive and ambition to succeed as you. I had to accept that, if a staff member was content to answer the phone all day, every day and that's all they wanted to do in life, then that was their calling. I had to learn to accept people for what they are.

Being driven is all well and good but as I have come to recognise, impatience is a flaw that must be overcome. All my staff members, apart from Elisa, were young and raw and for good reason. Even if some of my young personnel were less driven than I, they had not yet fallen into immovable traits that might not fit within my business model and philosophy. The young and untrained are the most receptive to being trained and moulded, not to mention they also command lower salaries. I'd rather build experience than buy it.

Within three months of working for DKM, I had my staff producing the desired results for the most part, which was a win-win situation for everyone. The staff were learning valuable lessons and techniques and I had them performing according to my standards without the need to pay senior rates. They, in turn, were making themselves more valuable in the market. In time they would achieve better results and salaries as a consequence of my training.

With my tight-knit team, I soon reached a turnover of $3 to 4 million per year, in an industry that typically required 15 to 20 staff members to achieve the same result. This is another important lesson to learn: keep it simple. If you follow this business model, you can achieve good results with a smaller payroll and thus become more profitable. The bottom line is on the profit and loss statement, not what your staff complement looks like. I was able to achieve this result with minimal staff by teaching them how to multi-task, which in turn added further to their own value and marketability. My staff learned new and valuable skill sets that don't just fall within the limits of their job description.

Right from the beginning DKM had an interest in China. As most of us know, if you can successfully operate a business with a Chinese connection, if you get that part of your operation established, there is good money to be made because you are able to import directly. As a direct importer, your margins will be much greater and, in the case of DKM, Shanghai was a part of the operation from Day One via a Chinese colleague with whom I had established a relationship.

I'd discovered the type of margins that could be made quite by accident back when I was working at Lina's company, Deep. One of our suppliers at that time sent me an email. About two minutes later he called, panicked and cried, "Delete the email. It's a virus. Delete the email. It's a virus."

I said, "Don't worry, I'll delete the email". However, I didn't delete the email. My curiosity got the better of me. I know now I took a real risk when I opened the attached spreadsheet. It was not a virus, fortunately. Instead, it contained their buying costs from a supplier in China.

I saw immediately they were making great margins. That was my first exposure to the possibilities that lay in doing business with China. It was my good luck to see that information but it was knowing how to use it to my advantage that has been one of the keys to my business success. That's when I started really delving into China.

When I first started DKM back in my parents' garden shed, I realised that if I got the China element correct it would make my business far more profitable than a standard promotional business. With over 2,000 competitors, I needed a key advantage. With that in mind, I flew to China to meet the agents and met a young kid, Jimmy, who was very new and inexperienced. I admired his passion to understand the business better. Consequently, when I arrived back in Australia, I spent a lot of time with him online teaching him everything I could. He spoke English fairly well, which was a massive asset; in fact it would later prove vital. I explained to him about products, the industry and what Australia is like because he had never been outside China.

I would come home late each night, head out to the garden shed, go online and we would cyber-chat for two to three hours. Eventually I suggested he leave his employer and set up his own company in China. He saw the opportunity with my Australian connection, which was the sales component, enabling him to focus solely on the supply component. To this day he is still one of my allies as his business grows, aligned with mine.

I flew Jimmy to Australia and spent time educating him about the values of the Australian market, the quality of products, and what was and was not acceptable. As a result he developed a clear understanding of my expectations and standards, and an appreciation of what I needed, as well as a more in-depth comprehension of the driving forces and market needs of DKM. Jimmy started out as a one-man operation in China and now has a dozen staff members. It gives me pleasure to see how successful Jimmy has become. It is in part as a result of our relationship that DKM is such a profitable operation.

As DKM merchandise is imported directly, it bypasses the middleman and minimises costs. No middleman also means faster, more responsive service across its range of more than 12,000 promotional items.

It also doesn't hurt to have Shanghai as one of the locations listed on the letterhead, emulating once again one of Richard Branson's techniques for success in making your operation look bigger than it is without being dishonest.

I had always thought it would be great for DKM to have an interstate presence. I knew I had a business trip coming up in Melbourne, so I started researching property prices on the internet.

I found one property I thought would be worthwhile checking out. It was an office on St Kilda Road, one of the main hubs of business in Melbourne, priced at $240,000. I called the agent for an appointment to inspect the property.

I knew that the property had been on the market for a year, so I figured I would offer something ridiculous to see if the buyer would bite. After reviewing the suite, I made an offer of just over half the asking price, $130,000. I said to the agent that if the owner agreed, I would confirm the purchase there and then. The agent laughed. There was no way, he said, the owner would go that low. I suggested the agent call the owner anyway, assuring him I was actually prepared to write a cheque for the full amount.

At the time there were numerous suites that were vacant in the building so I believed the ball was in my court. I suspected that, if the owner proved desperate, he would consider any offer on the table. I overheard the agent in the hallway as he spoke to the owner. To the agent's surprise and my delight, the owner accepted the offer.

Such is my luck or perhaps the lesson here is the value of chutzpah. In other words, if you don't ask the question, how will you give someone the opportunity to accept? OK, they could refuse but then you'd be no worse off than you were before you asked. In a nutshell, that is how Melbourne came to be added to the locations of DKM. From that point the DKM letterhead legitimately reflected locations in Sydney, Melbourne and Shanghai. It looked quite impressive for a total staff complement of five.

I pooled all my energy into building my brand. This effort was rewarded when, in 2005, the DKM logo was named by international logo ratings agency Logo Lounge as one of the world's most exceptional logos. DKM was on stage next to brands like Microsoft, GE, Intel and Bentley!

Logo Lounge has a booklet produced in New York every five years. My old friend and graphic designer, Corey Gross, was familiar with the publication, as being acknowledged by such a prestigious publication was something to which all designers aspire. Together we played around with a few ideas to submit for consideration, finally agreeing on a design that was then selected as among the top 2,000 in the world. Having one of the world's most exceptional logos may not appear to mean much but when your entire business is based on managing other people's images and profiles, it is vital to have some credentials on the board for your own image management before you can speak with credibility to others about managing theirs. That's when I came up with the slogan, "If we couldn't look after our own brand, how do you expect us to look after yours?"

Brand integrity is what we do. We can't say we are the market leaders and not take care of our own brand.

Of course I understand that it isn't just about winning awards. You could come up with the slickest logo design ever created but if the product behind it doesn't stack up, then you're not going to be able to take on the competition and gain greater market share. I understood, for example that if Sony, whose name and image is instantly recognisable, put their logo on a product that did not exude quality and the product fell apart the first time it was used, this would reflect badly both on the organisation and the product, even though that product might not have been actually manufactured by Sony and even though the product itself wasn't the product they were selling. The association would be there. If you allow your name, your brand image, your product or service, whatever it might be, to be associated with a poor quality end product, no matter how good your product might be, your image will be devalued.

I saw that the prevailing attitude in the merchandising business has always been to use the cheapest product available on which to put a logo. Competitors in the market believed if they kept products inexpensive, their clients would perceive this as value for money. To me the reverse was true. Why get a cheap product designed to last only a year or so in the marketplace and spend over a million dollars on a billboard campaign, which will last only a month, only to be wiped off with the next campaign? If you expose your brand with a lesser quality product, that product is going to tell a story about you for one, two, maybe three years. In all that time you are damaging your brand. Why would you cut corners on something as important as that?

I have found now that marketing managers are becoming more astute and starting to realise that they can drive their dollar further by using 'below the line marketing', which is also referred to as 'merchandising'. I identified this as an issue ahead of the pack and incorporated it into my philosophy from the first in my new business. Part of this philosophy crystallised while I was in Europe trying to consolidate my action plan to set myself apart from the competition. I set out to change the mentality of my industry and to that end began penning articles espousing my philosophy within trade magazines. Through perseverance, persistence and belief, DKM is now seen as a business of substance with exceptional standards and excellence in client service that my competitors in the market now have to match. Mine has become the benchmark in the industry.

Like Richard Branson in the airline industry, the vision which broke the mould has made me a market leader. Many people fantasise about leading the lifestyle of any of these market leaders but the reality is there are few with vision and even fewer prepared to put themselves out there and take the necessary risks. Success in any field of endeavour has never been achieved without taking risks. Climb to the peak of a mountain and there is generally a high velocity wind from those who covet your position ready to blow you off. If you want to rise to great heights, you must be prepared to put it all on the line and to protect your position once you arrive.

Entrepreneurial Strategies – Chapter Six

- Establish and build relationships with the best allies
- Hire young staff and train them in your image
- Keep it simple and don't overstaff
- Make your operation look as big as possible, without lying about it
- Compete for awards

Establish and build relationships with the best allies
Anyone and everyone who can help you achieve your objectives is a potential ally. Some are natural allies. For example, the people who share a common interest with you, the colleague who has been around for years and can offer an invaluable voice of experience, the team member who is always happy to be a sounding board for your ideas, or the vendor who is ready to accept seemingly impossible deadlines — these people are your natural allies. You can find allies in unexpected places too. Consider Arthur in finance, who pulls together an extra report on your project's finances; Sandy, the secretary, who tells you when the boss is in a good mood; or Fred, your ex-department head who is always available for advice — they are all important allies.

This is why it is imperative to be open and supportive to others in the workplace and why it is worth making an effort to help others out when they need it. If you're a positive and supportive person, most people will be equally supportive of you.

With more formalised alliances between businesses, there are some personal qualities that a business owner and alliance partner, like a supplier, should ideally possess:

- **Vision:** It is a bad idea to develop an alliance just because it seems to be the right thing to do or is in line with existing trends. It is essential to develop a mutually beneficial vision, along with the ability to look at the future prospects and not become dependent upon your alliance partner. However, if you become too independent, you may no longer need an alliance partner. You need to develop the vision to work towards creating successful alliances.
- **Curiosity:** Keep looking for new opportunities to raise profits and improve your capabilities. It pays to be open to new and unexpected opportunities and to be curious about alliance possibilities.
- **Communication:** Lack of communication can lead to the failure of an alliance. Every business owner should focus on transparency and effective communication.
- **Organisation:** Organising the alliance structure and procedures can have a huge impact on the longevity and ultimate implementation of the alliance. If the adopted alliance structure is complex, keep all details and documents organised. This helps to develop a long-lasting and profitable alliance.

- **Leadership:** Develop leadership that highlights your willingness to focus on getting things done, rather than an obsession for being right all the time. This will affect and determine the success of your alliance. This attitude should be present at the very start of your business.
- **Compassion:** Compassion, along with tolerance, should be maintained in an alliance. They help you to handle difficult situations and maintain your sanity.
- **Contracts:** Written agreements are vital to the success of an alliance, no matter how loyal and trusting each alliance partner is. Your expectations of one another and the promises you make should be documented and available for viewing whenever required.

Alliance relationships can be extremely profitable for all the parties involved. If you are confident and aware of all the steps involved, you will be well on your way. Of course that is but one form of alliance. Alliances useful to your business will come in many shapes and sizes.

"A problem shared is a problem halved", as the old saying goes and it is true in business as well. When working your way through the challenges you face every day, it is a great help to be able to draw on a network of supportive individuals to find solutions. Allies are the people who give you backing, assistance, advice, information, protection and even friendship. They comprise your support base. With strong, mutually beneficial relationships with your allies, you can survive and thrive in the corporate arena, enabling you to get things done more quickly and smoothly. Working together with allies helps you and they achieve more than if you worked independently.

Hire young staff and train them in your image
Let's say you are to undergo a recruitment drive. Do you hire people with the right attitude and train them with the skill set that best suits your business? Or do you hire those who have the skills but might have the wrong attitude? Personally, I prefer to hire younger candidates, who are open-minded and eager to learn. These individuals develop, grow, learn and appreciate your philosophies and work ethic to a greater degree.

Less experienced staff, I've found, can be trained up to speed in about three months. They don't demand the higher salaries and their enthusiasm and willingness to learn are, for me, more important to the business. I've developed my business with basically a team of juniors but they've been given the opportunity to grow and multi-skill. As the business has grown, I've complemented the younger employees with more experienced people. However, initially, my preference is for less experienced, enthusiastic staff. Part of my philosophy is to ensure that my staff are at their best. Training is a vital part of growth and development. Within my business it is crucial for me as their manager to ensure my staff performs at full potential. Where fitting, I encourage my staff to attend courses, which the company pays for, as I view it as an investment in their future as well as my business.

Keep it simple and don't overstaff
Small business owners run their companies like a ship's captain, retaining full decision-making power and control over the smallest details. But, as companies grow into larger enterprises with hundreds of employees and multiple product lines, the CEO's role must evolve as well. The CEOs of consistently successful companies give their subordinates a great deal of freedom to run their parts of the business.

There are some simple questions that can help uncover understaffing or overstaffing problems:
- Has the business model changed?
- Have there been major spikes in demand?
- Has the company gone through a round of layoffs?
- Is the company's overall productivity on target?
- Have skill levels changed over time?

Any good business management consultant will tell you not to overstaff merely to impress clients, friends or family. Your bottom line is your profit and loss statement, not your staff complement. While there are a plethora of critics against multi-tasking, in the early stages of your business development and perhaps even into the next level of your evolution, staff capable and willing to multi-task may not only be a benefit but could prove to be essential.

The most important point here is to grow your staff complement commensurate with your business needs, income and available capital; be flexible when it comes to considering part-time, casual and consultancy staff; but at the same time don't be penny-pinching and hold back on staff expansion when the genuine need does arise.

A big component to success is attributed to running a tight ship.

Do you have cash flow? Are your overheads too high? They are the factors you need to examine.

Don't overcapitalise on the assumption that your business is going to grow. Instead, once your business has grown, then spend the money. You've got to build the business one step at a time.

To enable me to run a tight ship, I have my staff multi-task wherever feasible. For example, all my salespeople are trained to complete costing sheets and purchase orders. I want them to know who the suppliers are and then I have them follow up the production. They can't be great salespeople if they don't know enough about production. A great salesperson can go into a meeting and answer questions on the spot. By multi-skilling, I can hire less staff. More importantly, it also means my employees are better informed as to how the business operates as a whole.

Make your operation look as big as possible, without lying about it

How you position your business is important. When I was starting DKM from the garden shed, I always tried to give the impression that I was a more established company in order to give people confidence when dealing with me.

Some of the ways you can 'fake it 'til you make it':

- **Always use the term 'we' rather than 'I':**
  One of the more subtle ways to look bigger than you actually are is to outsource your work and then refer to the outsourcer when talking to clients. If a client is asking you to complete some work and you say "I'll have to check with my designer to see when I can get that to you", it sounds a lot better than, "I'm really swamped this week, I'll try to get to it when I can". You also can say that you have several people working in your business.
- **Create a professional logo:**
  A professional logo is more than a want — it is a necessity. Your logo represents you and your company to customers and partners. A customer may never step foot into your office but they will definitely see your logo. The more professional it looks, the more professional you and your business look. If you don't have in-house expertise, someone at a logo design company can create a custom logo for your business. Start with your own idea or have

design experts create one for you. Once you have the right logo, the design company can apply it to business cards, stationery, signage and more.

- **Create a professional website:**
Having a website is a must for businesses today. A well-designed website can dramatically increase your business. Potential customers judge your business on both the design and functionality of your website. Also, ensure your content is grammatically correct and updated regularly. There are many web designers and online services to create and host savvy, professional sites at an affordable price. Remember, a well-designed website will attract new customers and keep old ones coming back. Design isn't the only consideration when creating a website. Make sure you have a respectable domain name, preferably your business name. Avoid using free sites to host your website as the website address will include the host site's name. Instead register your own domain name and pay for your website hosting through any one of the reasonably priced hosting sites. A good domain name offers credibility to your company and makes it easier for customers to find you when searching the web. You can find out more about hosting your website and registering your domain name online.

- **Developing professional marketing materials:**
  Like your website, your print materials should also be top-notch. There's no reason this must cost a fortune. Simple tactics such as using heavy paper or card stock, or glossy paper instead of matte, can make a two-colour print job look like a high-quality one. Freelance designers often design stationery, business cards and marketing materials for less than half the cost of a traditional advertising agency. In addition, you can save money by having the designer send you the final project files and then printing it yourself on a high quality, colour printer or copier.

- **Hire office space for important meetings:**
  Many small business owners work out of the home or in a one to two-room office, which isn't conducive for larger business meetings and presentations. But you can still have meetings with potential investors, vendors or customers over lunch or by renting meeting rooms in hotels or local office buildings. You can rent a meeting room for a specified number of hours a month for ongoing meetings and presentations. Renting a formal executive suite can give your company a professional appearance and make your business seem bigger than it is, while allowing for a temporary solution to spending big bucks on your own luxury meeting facility.

Using some of the above tips will help boost your business appearance while saving money. The best part is that you can work from home while projecting a professional image in keeping with your future membership in the Fortune 500!

Compete for awards
An often overlooked tool in your marketing toolbox is corporate awards or business awards marketing. Marketing consists of many techniques and channels from advertising and direct response to radio and trade shows. Take your small business to new levels by entering corporate awards. Corporate awards are operated by various profit and non-profit organisations to honour and recognise small businesses. At all levels, businesses have the opportunity to compete for corporate awards. Entering an awards program will usually require a brief essay and description of your business. Some contests require financials. The cost of admission may either be free or consist of a nominal charge.

"But I'll never win," you say. Entering corporate awards and contests as a marketing strategy is an untapped area by small business. With limited entries, your odds of winning improve. Even if you don't win, a title nomination can bring many rewards.

Selling your products and services in today's competitive marketplace is tough. A business award win or nomination can act as a third party endorsement.

The added credibility can even be used as a sales closer. A study of over 600 corporate award winners revealed winners had 37 percent more sales growth than non-winners. All companies profit from extra public relations. Awards are celebrations of achievement and hard work and a great story opportunity for the press to highlight small business. Not only that, but savvy employees want to work for the best companies. Corporate awards validate your hiring stature among new recruits.

Business awards offer many benefits to enhance your business's performance and profile and are definitely not something to shy away from. While not everyone can be a winner, half of the chance of winning is in the entering and, whether you win or not, the entire experience from penning the first word of the application to the awards ceremony and dinner can be an excellent reflective experience.

As the world's business environment becomes increasingly competitive and businesses question their return on investment for their marketing dollar, the strategic value of entering business awards can be an excellent way to gain a competitive edge over your competitors while increasing your profile and opening the door to further opportunities.

Hollywood stars vie for Oscars. Musicians vie for Grammys or Arias. So why shouldn't you, as an ambitious, driven, savvy business owner, vie for your slice of the accolades too? A win or nomination at the Oscars brings not only recognition of the highest accolade for acting talent, a solid future of movie contracts and larger earnings and even better, generally a massive box office bonanza worth an average of nearly $150 million. So why is it that time and time again small business owners shy away from business competitions? It's time to reconsider.

Notes

Chapter Seven

BRANDED: THINKING OUTSIDE THE BOX

One of my main goals has been to be perceived as a market leader. To this end I launched my own magazine, *Branded*.

Branded was an idea that came to me when I was speaking with the editor of *Marketing Magazine* during a tradeshow in Sydney. I was investing some money in advertising and wanted to push features and articles in their publication.

My aim is always to find how to invest next to nothing to generate something.

I was looking at ways to get exposure for my business and position myself as a market leader. I needed to put myself out there if I wanted to succeed. I came up with the idea of creating a magazine centred on the importance of branding. I wanted to redefine the way the industry was perceived in the marketplace and, in doing this, generate increased exposure for my business.

I intended to forge my position in the industry as a market leader in the branding, management and marketing arena. I wanted *Branded* to be a magazine that educated marketing managers about the importance of below the line marketing and branding.

After analysing the cost associated with the publication and how I was going to distribute it, we calculated that 16 pages would be the most cost effective size to produce and distribute. This would include a feature article written by me, some case studies and, to cover costs, some advertising space.

The overall cost of the publication was estimated to be $20,000 per issue. That included distribution, design, editing and printing 30,000 copies, making it the highest circulating magazine of its kind in the marketing industry. I piggybacked two leading publications and made *Branded* an insert in both. I arranged a group meeting with my key suppliers and pitched why they should advertise in my magazine. None of my suppliers sell directly; they rely on resellers to move their products to corporate companies. Their websites are generic ones that don't link back to their businesses. My angle was that this would provide a way for my suppliers to push their websites and products to end consumers, to force resellers to push their products. Eight advertisements at a rate of $2,500 for a full-page advertisement would cover my costs. My suppliers saw what I was trying to achieve and wanted to support my business just as I supported them. Funded through this advertising, my magazine became self-run with no expense to DKM, but it gave me scope to promote my philosophies and theories on business and share valuable case studies with consumers.

It was received with open arms and DKM's credibility soared as more and more marketers read the magazine. It was a quarterly magazine. I felt this frequency was ample. I didn't want to flood the market and tried to anticipate any pressure that my suppliers might have in their advertising spend.

I also knew there would come a point where suppliers would need to pull back on their investments. Eventually, suppliers couldn't measure a direct result of spending the amount of money I was charging, as there was no actual direct sell other than the promotion of their websites and a few product images. I emphasised to them they should see this as more of a brand platform position. I would need to work out how to show my suppliers a return on their investment. I revisited my initial concepts and decided to turn the magazine into a 'product-and-article' driven business. Instead of just making *Branded* a stand-alone magazine, I drew a direct link to DKM and made it a direct sales magazine instead. The marketing articles and my feature column remained. I began convincing suppliers that the measure of their return on investment through sales was linked directly to DKM, and, if they invested in a full-page advertisement of products then DKM would elevate them to the top priority supplier within their category. Indirectly, the message was that, if they didn't support the next phase of *Branded*, they could lose DKM's support of their business.

I looked at *Branded* like any commercial magazine publisher would. If you want to promote your product then you need to pay us for the advertising space to sell it. My focus now was to illustrate to my suppliers the maths behind their investment. If they took out a full-page advertisement, it would promote up to eight products. This would cost them eight cents for essentially 30,000 distributed copies, which was a very economical spend on advertising and, in my opinion, a sensible commercial decision on everyone's part. My first rollout with this new theory generated DKM $130,000 in new business. Our suppliers saw a direct link to sales as we could monitor the return on investment. Today, suppliers are soliciting me to request advertising space in *Branded*.

It was a real joy to see my ideas come to fruition. Believing in your theories and putting them into practice creates a strong sense of pride. Not every idea will work the way you expect it to, but you can't test your theories if you don't put yourself out there. *Branded* gave me the platform to put myself out there and voice my theories within an industry where I was determined to be a leader.

Branded was the first industry magazine to talk about the importance of marketing and branding and was yet another technique I found to redefine my position in the industry.

Entrepreneurial Strategies – Chapter Seven

- Piggyback other distribution channels
- Think outside the box
- Don't aspire to the market standards — create your own and raise the bar

Piggyback other distribution channels

There is no 'one size fits all' here. I was able to very successfully piggyback the distribution of my magazine, *Branded*, by inserting it in other magazines that already had a distribution channel in place. Production and distribution of the magazine ultimately derived from selling advertising space.

While there may be opportunities like this available to you if you consider your product or service and short, medium and long-term objectives, this particular idea may be completely inappropriate in your case. Accordingly, let's look at a few other forms of distribution.

A firm's distribution objectives will ultimately be related to services versus goods and high-end versus low-end markets. For example, more exclusive and higher service distribution will generally entail less intensity and lesser reach. Cost trades off against speed of delivery and intensity (it is much more expensive to have a product available in convenience stores than in supermarkets, for example). The extent to which a firm should seek narrow (exclusive) versus wide (intense) distribution depends on a number of factors. One such factor is the consumers' likelihood of switching brands and their willingness to search out new brands. For example, most consumers will switch soft drinks rather than walk from a vending machine to a convenience store several blocks away, so intensity of distribution is essential. Alternatively, if the product in question is sewing machines, consumers will expect to travel to a department or discount store and premium brands may have more credibility if they are carried only in full service specialty stores.

Retailers involved in a more exclusive distribution arrangement are likely to be more loyal, that is, they will tend to recommend that product to the customer and thus sell large quantities. In its early history, Compaq instituted a policy where all Compaq computers must be purchased through a dealer. On the surface, Compaq passed up the opportunity to sell large numbers of computers directly to large firms without sharing the profits with dealers. On the other hand, dealers were more likely to recommend Compaq since they knew that consumers would buy these from dealers. When customers came in asking for IBMs, the dealers were more likely to indicate that, if they insisted, they would sell them an IBM, adding, "But first, let me show you how you will get much better value with a Compaq".

Think outside the box

Don't struggle for a tiny niche. Instead, expand your horizons to create a whole new market opportunity.

The first principle is to reconstruct market boundaries to break from the competition. The challenge is to successfully identify how you can differentiate your business from your competitors. Don't compete on price but on your point of difference. DKM is different from other merchandising companies because we think like an ad agency rather than as a logo printing service. This is what makes us stand out.

The more companies compete on standard differentiators such as price, the greater the competitive convergence between them. To break out of stagnant waters, companies must break out of the accepted boundaries that define how they compete. Instead of looking within these boundaries, business owners must look systematically past such boundaries to create new opportunities.

They need to look across:
- alternative industries
- strategic groups
- buyer groups
- complementary product and service offerings, and
- the functional-emotional orientation of an industry.

This gives companies keen insight into how to open up innovative offerings in the market.

In the broadest sense, a company competes not only with the other firms in its own industry but also with companies in those other industries producing alternative products or services.

What are the alternative industries to your industry?

Why do customers trade across them?

By focusing on the key factors that lead buyers to trade across alternative industries and eliminating or reducing everything else, you can create a new market space for your business. How will you think outside the box today?

Don't aspire to the market standards — create your own and raise the bar

If you want to lead the market, you must be the industry leader in developing new business models and new products or services. You must be on the cutting edge of new technologies and innovative business processes. Your customer value proposition must offer a superior solution to a customer's problem and your product must be well differentiated. Also, you need to move faster than your competition! You must pursue the correct competitive strategy — avoid the strengths of your competitors and look for the weak points in their positions. Launch your marketing attacks against those weak points.

Sustainable competitive advantage is the prolonged benefit of implementing a unique, value-creating strategy based on a unique synergistic combination of internal organisational resources and capabilities that cannot be replicated by competitors. Sustainable competitive advantage allows the maintenance and improvement of your enterprise's competitive position in the market. It is an advantage that enables your business to survive against its competition over a long period of time. Do you want to encourage extraordinary performance from your people? Do you want them to do great things? If yes, then you must create an inspiring corporate culture to inspire and energise them.

Serving your market means that you are actively involved on the micro-level and have an obvious, vested interest in that market. It is going the extra mile to identify solutions and engineering innovative methods to deliver those solutions.

Obvious benefits to serving your market and becoming a market leader include: increased exposure, higher response and conversation rates and gaining unsolicited word-of-mouth referrals across the social media landscape. The latter is the best type of exposure possible.

Here are my keys to becoming a market leader:

- **Becoming a market leader is the end result, not the goal**: Becoming a market leader is not about having the largest mailing list, the highest-priced product or the biggest profit margin. Many businesses approach their market from that angle head on, not realising that these things are a result of market leadership. If you properly serve your market, then your list will naturally grow, and your products and services will ultimately be in higher demand. There is a difference between dominating your niche purely for gain and making every effort to truly serve your market. That difference is obvious to your clients and customers and it dictates whether your success will be long-term in that market — or a flash in the pan.

- **Become actively involved in your niche:** Be active on your own sites and also across the Web. Reply to emails. Respond to blog comments. Create social media profiles and actively participate. Join niche discussion forums and contribute value.

- **Create a customer follow-up strategy:** Go beyond making the sale and create a follow-up strategy that encourages your buyers to consume the material and to experience results. Your vested interest and continued support will turn those buyers into a loyal customer base.

- **Build a community, not a list:** Don't simply build a list you can constantly market to; instead, build a community within your target market. Being a market leader means being a market listener — and then taking action.

- **Follow market trends:** Don't be stale with your offer. Be proactive and move forward consistently — lead!

- **Don't respond, initiate:** While you should always respond to issues and conversations within your niche, you want to be the person to initiate those conversations whenever possible. Market leaders initiate relevant discussions.

- **Be proactive, not passive:** Reading a blog post is passive. Writing a blog post is active. Listening to podcasts is passive. Creating podcasts is active. Get actively involved in your niche by publishing content in a variety of formats across various media.
- **Communicate frequently:** Don't email your list only when you have something to sell them. Provide quality content on a regular basis to stay fresh in their minds. Serving your market consistently will build rapport and trust with them.

- **Act on feedback:** Show appreciation for the feedback you receive by taking action on it. Acknowledge complaints and make necessary changes. While you don't want to become a slave to your market, you should open yourself up to serving that market when they make it a point to let you know how you can best do that.

How many of your competitors follow even half of the points on this list? How many of these points are you using in your own business model? Take these ideas and dominate your niche, simply by better serving your market.

Notes

Chapter Eight

REBIRTH OF AN IDOL

Success is not for the faint-hearted and in all things there is universal and cosmic balance. If you are not grateful for the success you achieve, not just in recognising your friends and those who helped you along the road but in giving back to others in some meaningful way, you may discover that something will reverse your good fortune. I was determined this wasn't going to happen to me.

In 2004, I realised I needed to seek ways to differentiate myself from the competition. I felt one way I could do this was to extend the concept of branding merchandise to brand management by offering the kind of celebrity management services we are familiar with in the arena of sports and entertainment.

I wanted to stay involved in basketball and thought if I could become a player agent/manager, I could use my contacts in the sport to attract clients. Other than my common sense in business I didn't really know anything about being an agent. I don't know why I keep on throwing myself into the deep end and placing myself in situations I don't really know anything about.

The first player I managed was Kavossy Franklin, a highly talented American import who was part of the Sydney Kings first championship team. Through the sport, we knew a common friend who confided to me that Kavossy needed representation in Australia as he hadn't been re-signed with the Kings for the following year. Kavossy and I met. Following our conversation, he was keen to see what I could do for him. He was out of contract for one year and was anxious to come back to Australia and continue his career. He was looking for anyone who could help him secure a job. As I wouldn't get paid if I was unable to secure him a contract, I didn't present a risk to him. I did shop Kavossy around to a few NBL clubs and generated some interest from The Hunter Pirates, who were based in Newcastle. This was my first experience with contract negotiation in the sporting arena. Even though I was a little bit nervous I was excited to see what sort of deal I could negotiate. Kavossy had indicated he wanted more money than what he was getting from the Sydney Kings. I managed to negotiate a deal that would earn him $30,000 more. Needless to say Kavossy was more than happy with the contract.

Not only did I manage to negotiate more money but I also managed to sign up his college teammate from New Mexico, Clayton Shields. I had a college highlight reel that was four years old and used this to secure Clayton's deal.

Chapter Eight | Rebirth of an Idol

Clayton hadn't played in over two years, so he was excited to be restarting his career. However, I was a bit scared as I was negotiating a deal on someone I hadn't seen firsthand and who had retired two years earlier. I had reservations about whether Clayton could in fact live up to expectations based on his college achievements. Unfortunately, a pre-season knee injury ended his hopes and we never did find out how well he might have performed.

From then on, I didn't need to go searching for players to represent. Calls from Division One college players began coming in after Clayton spread the word. If I could sell Clayton based on old tapes, then these players wanted me to represent their interests. While I dabbled in this area of sports management for a little while, I didn't push it any further as I felt it required too much work for too little long-term loyalty to make this a worthwhile business. Instead, I redirected my focus back to merchandising and branding.

Then with the explosion of the hit television programme, *Idol,* onto the world stage, a new and very different opportunity came my way. The show has launched many new careers globally. In Australia, as in other countries, hopefuls flocked to the auditions. Of those who did make it through, we saw astonishing, previously unrealised talent in our youth, but there is only one winner. What happens to the others? Some runners-up have gone on to enjoy success in the performing arts, having realised their life's calling. How many of them,

I wondered, fell prey to the hungry sharks that circled, waiting to pick off the cast-offs and the unwary?

One evening I was at my friend's restaurant when I was introduced to Cosima De Vito. Cosima had appeared in the first season of *Australian Idol* as a top three finalist and famously pulled out of the competition just before the final voting because of nodules in her throat.

On the back of the show she went on to win an ARIA award and was the first independent artist to debut at No. 1 on the charts, with her single, When the War is Over, which achieved Platinum sales. Her first album went on to achieve Gold sales accreditation.

I suggested she should look at doing some merchandise, reasoning there could be some good opportunities for her. Cosima was there with her sister, Sarina, so I gave Sarina my card. I spoke with her a week later and organised a meeting. Cosima had started up her independent label called CDV Records and my focus was on the merchandise possibilities of her career. An initial half-hour merchandising discussion stretched into a two-hour meeting, which spilled over into dinner and ultimately became a six-hour session. It was immediately apparent to me that there was a great deal more to Cosima than I had read about in the press. Her relationship with her manager, she revealed, was becoming strained.

What I knew about the music industry could have been written on a postage stamp but I did know about running a business and managing a brand. Before long we agreed that I would start consulting with her on the business front. For the first time, I wasn't doing this work for any immediate gain; I simply felt sorry for her situation because she was raw in the business arena.

It was December 2004. We let the holiday season pass before settling down to any meaningful work. Then I began asking some serious questions.

When I asked Cosima later how I managed to earn her trust to step into such a pivotal position in her life, she told me that at the start she didn't like me; she thought I was arrogant. However, after the first meeting she said my apparent honesty changed her opinion. I wasn't trying to exploit her for money. Looking back, I calculate that I've probably spent more money on her career than I've made. Any other manager relying on her for an income would have left a long, long time ago. I could see there was a lot more there than met the eye, things that other people either didn't know about, didn't understand, or simply didn't care about.

There were times I did ask myself what I had gotten into but I am not a quitter. Even if this wasn't about making money, it was about helping another human soul, which was rewarding and about challenging my own boundaries, which was enriching.

Whether it is music or selling a product, the same business principles apply. These include managing your overheads, outgoings and incomings. Selling an artist is no different from selling a tangible product. Tangible or intangible, you still need to entice the consumer. Be it a song, an album, a photo, or a garment, the same principles apply. Once Cosima's massive outgoings were slashed, there came a point when her business interests were run out of my office and from there it was a short step for Cosima to ask me to manage her. There had been over a million dollars spent on producing and promoting Cosima's first album after *Australian Idol*. Cosima was not from a wealthy background; in fact her parents had gone into debt to raise the money to support her dream. They didn't understand what the expenditures were for but assumed that, if people were spending that much money on Cosima, surely the returns would be enormous. The reality was the complete reverse.

When I looked at all her invoices and saw what was being charged, I was staggered at how much money had been spent on public relations, promotions, rent, etc.

It was a learning curve for us both. For me, it was learning about the music industry. For Cosima, it was learning how to run her business and regain her belief that some people in business do have integrity. Even though I lacked knowledge and experience in the music industry, I had managed sports athletes before and I wasn't without connections in the music business through various friends. I began managing Cosima's expenses as well as her brand. I was testing my own abilities to see how far I could push my own boundaries in venturing into this new world. Perhaps the biggest challenge was managing a four-year legal battle against Cosima's ex-manager who was suing her for commissions and royalties of $500,000.

I involved my own lawyers, which was not an inexpensive exercise. Together with Cosima, we worked out a plan. We knew Cosima's ex-manager didn't stand a chance. Finally, after four years of heartache, the judge ruled in Cosima's favour with only a bill of $40,000 to be paid for his unpaid work. Only then could she finally speak out, through exclusives in *New Idea* magazine and explain what had taken place.

The public battle did take its toll on Cosima's career and, for a long time, even though both Cosima and I knew there was light at the end of the tunnel, that tunnel seemed awfully, interminably long.

In my role as Cosima's manager, life is now about putting the blocks back in place to rebuild her career and, while there is unlikely to ever be the hype around her that there once was in the days of *Australian Idol*, she's still attracting a lot of fresh media interest. The difference is that now it's all positive. In recent times, I secured her gigs with the legendary Demis Roussos, the hit musical *Hair* and booked her on a Rocheford tour. Momentum has returned.

This enabled me to manage the production of Cosima's second album, which we called, *This Is Now*. We worked on a budget of $100,000 compared to the million dollars squandered on her first album. My strategy behind the second album was ultimately to get Cosima back in the marketplace with a fresh new start and for us to create a bit of hype to generate corporate and live performances. The intention was never to work toward record sales; after all she wasn't coming off the back of the television show. I elected to produce a much smaller release of the overall album, 4,000 as opposed to 75,000 as she had done with her first. I wasn't looking at CD sales but at other areas. To date, we've recouped the album costs with live performances. We haven't sold a million records but we're slowly and surely transforming her into a contemporary adult artist who is respected for her vocal talent.

Cosima has penned six songs for her second album, making it infinitely more rewarding. She now feels a part of the entire process. Under my guidance and management, she has grown both as an artist and an individual and developed a positive focus towards the bright future ahead. As well as managing her, I have taken it upon myself to motivate her even though many people around me told me I was wasting my time and money. However, those critics don't know the real Cosima and couldn't possibly understand what we have gone through together as a team. Once again, they were selling me short on my vision and belief — and they've been wrong before. It has been a real test, both emotionally and financially but how can one put a price on keeping the dream alive?

At the moment the focus is on securing Cosima an income through live performances. All the emotional baggage has been left behind and we are adopting the philosophy of the old saying, "What doesn't kill you makes you stronger". We have both learned and grown through the tumultuous experience of a prolonged, high profile lawsuit. Along with this we have bonded as friends who respect each other's knowledge of our respective fields.

Despite the roadblocks thrown up, we took the first step back to restoring the fallen idol on her throne. Even when small things started to go well, I would keep Cosima grounded while maintaining my encouragement and positive attitude towards the future. I taught her how to look at everything from a business perspective, something she'd never done in the past.

The change in Cosima's brand is how we secured a national tour with Demis Roussos, a ten-time platinum artist. Performing at the Opera House and every other major venue around Australia has been a wonderful experience for Cosima. Even more amazing was that at the Opera House she was able to perform a song that she wrote when she was 11 years old, *Forever Young*.

Cosima explains how much this tour meant to her: "I remember when we did the Demis Roussos tour; Dorry took me to the office and said, 'I've got a surprise for you'. He knew my Dad used to play his Demis Roussos album when I was a baby and there was a song called *Smile*, written by Charlie Chaplin that I would sing along to. Every time I would cry, Dad would rock me in his arms to Demis Roussos. Anyway, between Dorry and the promoters, they spoke to Demis and told him this story, asking him if he would be prepared to sing a duet with me and he said 'absolutely'. So there I was, on stage with a man who I have idolised my entire life, singing *Smile*. I didn't think it could get any better than that but after the tour had finished, Dorry gave me a blow-up of the Demis Roussos Opera House poster on an enormous plaque. He was so proud of it and I thought it was an absolutely amazing gesture. After that, everything just flew. I headlined the musical *Hair* in Perth for three weeks, which was a sell-out show. Not only was it a sell-out but the show was actually extended. And if that wasn't enough, Dorry negotiated a deal whereby I would earn a certain amount per show plus a bonus based on ticket sales which, combined, equated to an amount approximately seven to eight times what the other headline acts were making."

"We did the second album on a tenth of the budget of the first because, when it comes to negotiating, Dorry is absolutely fierce. The producer on it was Trevor Steel, who used to be with The Escape Club and most of the songs I recorded on it I'd written myself because Dorry told me I had to make money from this second album and to do that, they had to be my own original songs. So that's what I did. I wrote most of the album and when the first single, *Keep it Natural*, was released as a dance version, we gave it to all the clubs and I debuted in the ARIA dance charts as a result."

Cosima charted in both the Independent ARIAs as well as the ARIA Dance arena with her track *Keep it Natural* like there was no tomorrow. The gay community welcomed that track into their clubs with open arms and hearts and the album started to sell in record numbers. I had recognised this as a niche market for Cosima and worked it. Releasing dance tracks off the album really worked wonders. Through 2007 and 2008, Cosima became a much beloved gay diva, headlining the Sleaze Ball which, after Mardi Gras, is the second biggest gay party in Sydney. She retains her popularity as one of the much-loved artists within the gay community and that is all because I said I wanted Cosima to develop a niche market.

Cosima has been the first independent artist to debut at number one with *When the War is Over*, which actually came off her first album but she didn't receive the award until 2005, when she was under my management. I escorted her to the ARIA No. 1 Chart Awards and she handed me the award to keep in my office as a thank you for my support.

I adopted a specific and deliberate strategy concerning Cosima's second album. I knew Cosima's income stream would come predominantly from live performances. I would negotiate a fee for each performance equal to what she might earn for an estimated 1,000 album sales. Behind this rationale was the knowledge that all the hype from the TV show had been well spent. Yes, we needed product in the form of recordings for leverage at the performances to create credibility for Cosima as an artist and demand for future performances, but the strategy remained firm to sell Cosima as a live act, of which the product sales would come off the back.

Success isn't always a monetary thing. It's not about selling a million records. It can also be defined as facing challenges and working through obstacles. We faced a lot of challenges in that area and we overcame them. Not everything you do is going to be outrageously successful. However, if your actions are undertaken with integrity and quiet confidence, you are moving ahead on the right track. Success is measured in many ways. Whether it's a small achievement or a big achievement, it's an achievement. The aim is to test yourself and to push beyond the barriers of perceived limitation. It's about having small goals and conquering them step by step.

People who know me, know I like to socialise and think it's a good form of business networking. Here I am with my brother David.

DKM Christmas parties have become a big social gathering for our clients and staff, and are growing bigger every year.

Ernst & Young Entrepreneur of the Year awards dinner with my close friend Harry Cousens.

*Celebrating with my loving family.
Left to right: My sister Christine, Mum, myself and Dad.*

Wayne Taylor/FairfaxPhotos

My first major signing. Highly regarded US Import Kavossy Franklin.

Overleaf:
The Last Dance: Our Game Five of the NBL grand final, Sydney Kings vs. Melbourne Tigers. The game sold out the Sydney Entertainment Centre two hours before tipoff. This brought back memories as to where basketball should be.

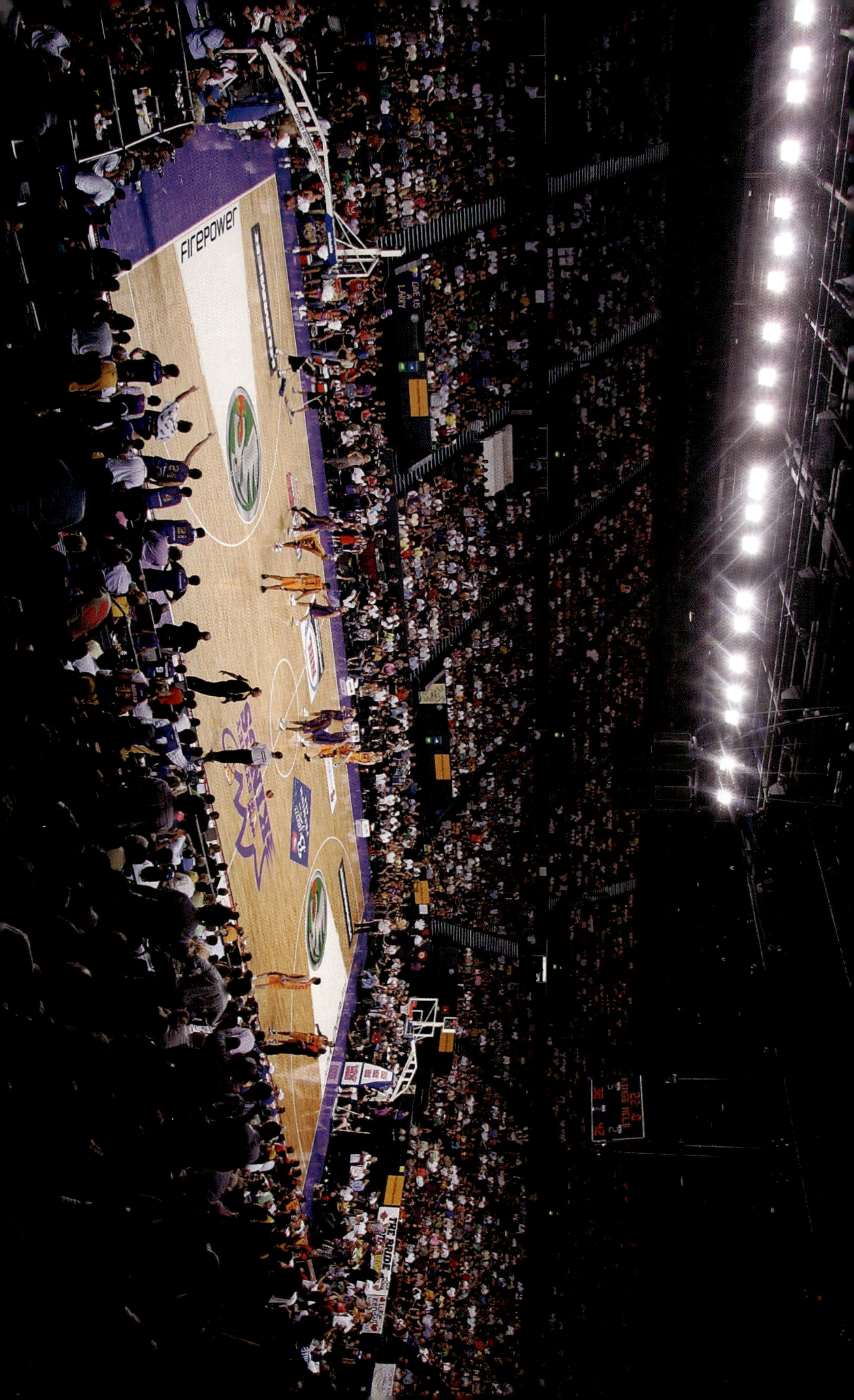
FirePower

DKM courtside branding at the Sydney Entertainment Centre.

Courtside with international singing sensation Patrizio Buanne.

In China with Brian Goorjian, a man I respect and to whom I am still very close.

Rebranding an Australian Idol, Cosima De Vito.

The magazine I launched to give me the edge in the heavily competitive market of merchandising.

Entrepreneurial Strategies – Chapter Eight

- Create your own benchmarks
- Be grateful and give back
- What doesn't kill you makes you stronger
- Branding is art, not a science

Create your own benchmarks

If you want to lead the market, you don't have to follow what is currently the standard practice. Do what you think is right. When I started DKM nobody was servicing the merchandising business the way we do. We fit in between an advertising agency and a promotional company, without the fees of an ad agency. That makes us unique. People said it couldn't be done that way, but I knew I was right, so I followed that path.

As I said earlier, you should strive to be the industry leader in developing new business models and new products or services. Your customer value proposition must offer a superior solution to a customer's problem and your product must be well differentiated. Also you should move faster than your competition!

A market leader stands apart from other solution providers in their niche simply by listening more, providing higher quality, leveraging various elements in the market and simplifying processes. The bottom line is to become the 'go to guy' in your industry and to establish trust and rapport with your target market.

One of the keys to becoming a market leader is to examine your competition and determine what they are doing right. How can you do it better? Even more powerful is to determine what they are doing wrong (or not doing at all) and then to capitalise on that space between them and the market.

Be grateful and give back
You don't have to be Bill Gates and donate millions of dollars to charity to give back. To be grateful in life, all you have to do is to stay alert, watch your surroundings and not take life for granted.

Particularly once you become successful, you've got to stay humble and do things that are not always about money. With Cosima my initial motivation was simply to help someone I could see was in trouble. By doing that I've gained so much in terms of broadening my experience. You've got to learn to take on challenges and to keep pushing yourself beyond your boundaries. The moment you get complacent is the moment you stop growing.

What doesn't kill you makes you stronger
How often do we let the little things get in our way? In the course of our own existence, we each encounter devastating losses, heartbreaking experiences and tumultuous issues. In those moments, when our concentration is focused on overcoming obstacles or

coping with loss, we may be distracted from recognising what we can achieve. Feelings of loss only occur when there is an appreciation for the thing that is lost. You cannot lose what you never had. Understanding what you can attain may cause frustration when encountering delays, but do not allow temporary interruptions to distract you from your personal goals. Learn from the obstacles and adjust accordingly. Once the grieving over the loss has subsided, there is a period of peace where you can remind yourself of what you can achieve. Small setbacks are insignificant in comparison to what you can accomplish and should never dissuade you from your course of action.

Most of our disappointments are the result of discovering that expectations or assumptions we had were incorrect. Occasionally, the realisation may have life-changing consequences. It is common to encounter such challenges in relationships, careers and personal development. Study the obstacles presented to you and adjust your course accordingly. In taking a new path, you will inevitably encounter new discoveries that you would otherwise have missed, both in the environment around you and within yourself. By overcoming a seemingly venomous situation, you could make a monumental personal discovery for yourself. Temporary setbacks and challenges cannot beat you but you can use them to make you stronger. Everyone has heard the axiom, "Necessity is the mother of invention", meaning that, if everything was status quo in everyone's lives all the time, there would be no progress or development in medicine, in technology, in philosophy or even in interpersonal relationships. Think of how many relationships have grown stronger through shared adversity.

There are countless examples of historical and global significance where almighty diversity has led to monumental and positive developments. But, on an individual level, it's suffice to say that the mind is stronger than anything, so much so in fact that it does have the ability to either kill you or make you stronger. Developing inner strength is what is directly responsible for developing outer strength. If a challenge is sent to you to overcome, don't walk away from it or you'll never know what treasures lay behind the door you forever left unopened.

Branding is art, not science

I believe brands are one of the most, if not the most, important assets for any business. I can understand why finance departments want to measure their value. But there is an important point that the whole 'value' argument misses: brands are all about emotional responses, things such as trust, confidence, image and values. You can't measure these things.

Recently an Albert Namatjira painting sold for more than $80,000. Would any rational accountant have placed such a value on this item? No, of course not. It's art.

People pay for art based upon how it makes them feel. They pay because art evokes an emotional response and people place value on the experience of feeling emotion.

An artist, especially one like Cosima, is all about the emotional connection they make with their audience. An executive at a record company might measure the value of an artist in terms of record sales. But this misses the point.

For example, when Cosima was a special guest for Demis Roussos's national tour and performed at venues such as the Opera House, there was obviously a hard commercial value that could be drawn from the event. There was an appearance fee plus the chance to build profile and CD sales.

But these transactions were not directly linked to Cosima's value as a performance artist. Her value is immeasurable because it begins and ends with the emotional response Cosima's performance evoked within each individual member of the audience.

How do you measure that?

The work I do at DKM with brand management is exactly the same. The value of a brand is wholly contained within the emotional response it solicits from its audience. That is their essence. That is why brands are so incredibly valuable.

Some business leaders judge anything which cannot be reduced to a financial transaction as having no value. But this hard-line perspective is their limitation, not a limitation on the part of professional brand managers. If a CEO or CFO sees no value in their brands, then it is their loss; ultimately their brand values will be eroded and their whole business will wither accordingly.

I couldn't put a hard dollar value on what I experience when I hear a live performance by a great artist. Whatever it costs to attend, to me it's worth it. Would I resell my ticket for $500, or even $100? Even thinking about the emotional value in this way alters my perspective and diminishes the experience somewhat.

Marketing and brand managers typically have an intrinsic understanding of the value and importance of brands. All the hyper-rational talk about fixing exact dollar values to brands does not help define brand value except for those executives who only think in terms of hard currency.

We could argue that if 'they don't get it', it is their problem. But that is ultimately defeatist. We all have to work together. We are all on the same team. At the end of the day everyone, from the most junior right up to the most senior, is measured by the overall performance of their organisation.

I strongly believe that we marketing managers should be referred to as relationship managers. As custodians of our brands, we are the ones ultimately responsible for ensuring everyone is rallying to protecting our standard and winning new ground.

Notes

Chapter Nine

THE SYDNEY KINGS

For me building success is always challenging but even more challenging is maintaining it. As I've said before, I have always had a passion for basketball and the Sydney Kings was the team that I loved as a child.

I think most men dream of being associated with a sport in some shape or form. I was fortunate to follow my dream and have a crack at investing in one. Do I think it was a money-maker? Of course not! Did I think I would lose money doing this? Of course I did.

It was at a time in my life when I had accumulated some personal wealth and the sport was going backwards. I knew that certain clubs were going through tough times. I made a call to a friend and ex-player, Derek Rucker. That call led to a meeting with Robbie Cadee, CEO of the West Sydney Razorbacks. Robbie had been there for ten years and was a veteran of the sport. We struck up an instant rapport but even after Robbie understood my vision, for various reasons it didn't look like I was going to invest in the Razorbacks. Instead, discussions progressed to see how I could make this happen with the second Sydney team, the team where my heart really belonged, the Sydney Kings. I hadn't believed the Kings would be interested in investors hence my focus on the Razorbacks. In fact a deal was nearly struck with the Razorbacks but I was pipped at the post by another investor who got in ahead of me. Thinking that the mix would never work, I was ready to forget the whole thing when I received a call from Derek saying the Kings wanted to talk. Having always had a soft spot for the purple and gold, I didn't need to be asked twice.

Negotiations began looking positive. It was clear to everyone this was potentially a good marriage of skills and experience. Tim Johnson owned the team and I took a 10 percent share.

I knew I would lose money and I knew how much money I was willing to lose to live out a dream. Even though I knew I would not make money directly through the sport I had an idea that I could use the professional sporting arena as a vehicle to diversify into other corporate environments, cross-pollinate my business and make them leverage off each other.

People thought I was mad investing in the team and said it was a waste of time; I agree they were right on one level, but they didn't understand what I was trying to create.

I looked at my investment as a marketing exercise. The perks I had with my part-ownership included promoting my company through courtside advertising,

Chapter Nine | **The Sydney Kings**

courtside corporate boxes and displaying my logo on all team uniforms and merchandise products. I was able to manage and purchase the stock through my business. I was also able to promote my artist, Cosima, during warm-up and game time as part of the entertainment schedule. At the very least, if I entertained corporate clients and networked through the channels of the Kings, I would likely gain business from the endeavour and give my company, DKM, exposure. I started putting DKM everywhere and leveraging off each of my networks and brands to benefit the others.

It's natural for me to look at ways and possible opportunities to help any part of my business to grow through my ventures. This appeared to be a win-win scenario for both me and my business.

I received a phone call from the team's coach, Brian Goorjian, welcoming me and saying how excited he was to have me on board. I have a lot of respect for Brian. He is one of the most motivational people I have ever encountered and has the funniest personality. There are not many people who can tell a joke over and over again and still draw a laugh. He is, in my opinion, the greatest coach in the history of the NBL and the friendship we built up over the year still endures.

Brian had this to say about his time with the Sydney Kings:

"When the Kings changed ownership, from this time on, the uniforms for the players, the practice games, the training facilities, the contracts and the promotion of the game were bad. I had been around for a long time so I was naturally concerned at what I was seeing. It is my recollection that it was about that time Dorry walked into my life."

"There was no one from the ownership around us, there was no support, there was no anything and then all of a sudden Dorry walked through the door and I was told that he was going to be part of the ownership of the team. From the moment I met him, in all honesty, he provided me comfort. Here was a guy that was young, full of energy, positive, very intelligent, motivational, innovative and charismatic. If you had a business contact you could be confident that Dorry could talk about any subject. He was confident, he was comfortable with himself and he was impressive."

"He could relate to the players because he'd been a player himself. He would make you feel positive, even when the environment was negative. He was a *can do* guy. If Dorry was buying uniforms, you knew they were going to be good quality. If attendance numbers were down, he had a four-pronged approach to build the numbers back up. I remember an unbelievable Christmas party with a lot of high flyers around. He brought many impressive people to the game. You could tell he was connected; he was a mover, he was aggressive. He was unbelievably positive in a completely negative environment, assuring us we were going to be okay, explaining what we were going to do in marketing and he was always at the

Chapter Nine | The Sydney Kings

games with high energy talking about the plans to move forward."

All this was new territory for me and I was determined to cherish every moment of this and learn from it. At the first training session I attended Brian introduced me to the team. We had a championship team with five Olympians in our squad. I introduced myself and gave the players some background on me, as this was a first meeting for most of us. I was the same age as most of these young players, so I had to try and earn their respect. Over the weeks I focused on building trust with Brian and the players. Actions speak louder than words in my book and I made every effort to ensure my actions spoke of my full support.

I invited family and a few close friends to sit in my courtside box at the first home game. I had a smile from ear to ear throughout the entire game thinking to myself this is one of the most unbelievable moments of my life. Apart from the nerves, the experience was both exhilarating and surreal. I kept thinking about how far I had come in such a short time and all the obstacles I had overcome to get me to this point. To share this experience with family and friends gave me a true sense of pride. My passion for the sport had brought me to this place that I created for myself, a place where I knew I was going to make a difference.

I have never forgotten the excitement that raced through my young veins when I was a towel boy for the Sydney Kings and part of me always dreamed of owning a piece of that club if I couldn't play for them professionally.

The 2007/08 season was one of the most challenging years in the history of the Sydney Kings and it was this year that, by the season's end, we folded. I had been there at both the birth and the crucifixion of the Kings. Despite all the off-court drama, we managed to finish minor premiers and have the second best record in the history of the NBL with 27 wins and three losses.

How did it all go pear-shaped? It started with our major shareholder walking away from the team and his heavy investment. After that, each month it was a battle to stay afloat, with funds deposited into the accounts at the eleventh hour. The experience was probably the most challenging one I have ever encountered. To finish minor premiers was amazing, particularly considering all the off-court difficulties as things crumbled. Credit must be given to Brian, the coaching staff and the players. I did my best to support both the players and coaching staff, but I could see where it was going. As a minority holder, however, there was little I could do. For someone who prefers to be in control, it was difficult to accept that I could not fix what was wrong.

One of my rules I live by now is that I will not invest in something I cannot control. If I cannot control the situation I don't want to be a part of it. If I am going to fail I want to fail off my own abilities not off someone else's.

Chapter Nine | The Sydney Kings

At my very first board meeting, just one week after I invested into the team, I could see there were serious issues that needed tackling. I was determined to view this as a challenge, not as an insurmountable problem.

It was at this meeting that I met Harry Cousens, a former Kings owner. We soon became good friends.

Harry was Sydney-born and bred, educated in a public school and entered the computer industry at a very young age. It was he who initiated Dell Computers' presence in Australia in 1993, which in turn led to other opportunities, until he retired from the corporate world in 2000 (coincidentally on the day the Olympics started in Australia). His retirement had been intended to be a six-month sabbatical but he never went back. At the age of 42, he decided he'd prefer to just enjoy his life, get to know his kids and relax. He looked around at possible investment vehicles. One of those was sport. Harry is an absolute sports fanatic with favourite teams in every sport.

Coincidentally, his cousin, Mike Wrublewski, had started the Sydney Kings in 1988 and so the family had a fondness for the team. Harry explains his involvement in the club:

"It was always a great night out with the kids. Saturday and Sunday nights we'd take the children to the Entertainment Centre. It became a family tradition so when an opportunity came past my nose regarding the then ownership group in 2004, to see if I would like to buy 10 percent of the club, I couldn't ignore it. I knew

153

it wasn't a great financial investment; it was more of a lifestyle investment. When my friends asked, 'Ever think about buying a boat?' I'd say, 'No, I have a basketball team instead'. A boat wastes about the same amount of money as owning a sports team but, to me, it was much more enjoyable. It was rewarding in many other ways too, such as growing my network and getting to make very close friends with the likes of Brian Goorjian and Bill Tomlinson, the coaches of the club. We won three titles, so that was very satisfying, too."

"It was then that our CEO, Gordon Allen, who had realised the club was in financial difficulties, was looking for some other financial investors. Dorry was introduced to us. That was about September or October 2006. I met Dorry at his office the very first time when Gordon Allen organised a meeting between me, Tim Johnston, some of his people and Dorry. I thought as Dorry was running a successful business he could be an asset to the club. Of course he didn't know me from a bar of soap and I didn't know who this young boy was but very soon we became very, very close friends. We bonded. We found each other to be honest and had common interests, chiefly in wanting to see the Kings do well. Even though those were tough times, Dorry knew what he was getting himself into and as he'd turned his own life around so remarkably to succeed in business I thought, well why can't he do it with basketball? Most people who love sport think they know how to run a sports team. Let me tell you that very few people know how to run a sports team. Sport is one of the toughest businesses to make money in and the quality of sports management in this country is, in my opinion, abysmal. This is why we see a lot of sports entities in big trouble."

As enjoyable as the season was, it was also equally frustrating. I had no control over changing the issues I felt needed changing. I could see that things were going south but was powerless to stop this happening. Our back office was in disarray, our corporate sponsorship was minimal and ticket sales were average. A lot of people involved seemed content just to be there, without rolling up their sleeves and getting their hands dirty. No one seemed to want to turn things around. Maybe they were simply out of their depth.

Our on-court performance was the best it had ever been. Brian had the team in sync and our early season trip to China to compete against Yao Ming and the Chinese national team, CSKA Moscow and Benetton Treviso, was a turning point for the team. It instilled in us the belief that we could compete on the world stage against the best teams in Europe. This trip away was, for me, a poignant time. Childhood fantasies have a way of weaving their way into our adult lives. Here I was, sitting on the team bench, part of the Sydney Kings. Admittedly, it was not as a player, but to be present in that moment as a shareholder is a feeling I hope I never forget.

Don't forget, you never know where that spark of magic is secretly lurking until you find the key to unlock that door. Just stop and think before you continue through this chapter: what secret passion burned inside you as a child?

We were on the verge of winning the title. I was thrilled that we might win a title during my first season as a shareholder. It was regarded as one of the best series ever played. In Game Four, we came back from 22 points down to take it to Game Five at the Sydney Entertainment Centre. Sadly though, we went down in Game Five of the grand final against the Melbourne Tigers. Injuries gave way and we lost in the final minutes. Regardless, it was one of my most memorable nights to date. Two hours before tip-off, we were sold out, 10,500 seats in the Sydney Entertainment Centre. The atmosphere was electric with the Sydney community coming together in support of the Kings. It was still a perfect ending to a season that many suspected would be the last.

At the season's end, serious issues began to arise. Players were no longer being paid once our major investor walked away. The media got a sniff of this and before we knew it, the liquidators descended and seized the business to recoup what they could. I lost some money but I had been prepared for that.

Harry and I went into survival mode, attempting a rescue plan to raise $1.5 million to keep the team alive but, after three weeks, we were still $600,000 short. I'm proud of what we managed to do in such a short time but unfortunately it wasn't enough.

Chapter Nine | **The Sydney Kings**

Towel boy's bid to save Sydney Kings

By Tim Morrissey
From: *The Daily Telegraph*
June 24, 2008 12:00AM

A FORMER Sydney Kings towel boy is putting together a business plan to revive the team he once wiped the sweat off the floor for — but has just 48 hours to do it.

Dorry Kordahi is behind a bid to buy the Kings and save the club from NBL extinction.

Kordahi has remained a passionate Kings fan since his court-wiping days in the 1990s and, with his business partner Harry Cousens, is behind a last-ditch bid to save them.

He held a 10 percent stake in the franchise owned by Tim Johnston, who has vanished, leaving a trail of debt and despair since the club's catastrophic collapse.

Like the unpaid players, coaches and staff, Kordahi, who owns a marketing company, was also badly burnt financially by Johnston, but has been working frantically with Cousens to put a rescue package together.

Cousens, a successful businessman in his own right, was also a previous Kings owner with the consortium that sold the club licence to Johnston.

The pair have raised close to $1 million but need to find some more investors to bring in a further $600,000 if they are going to have a legitimate shot at taking over the Kings' licence. "The business plan is there, the NBL has been encouraged by what we've been able to put together in just four days," Kordahi said.

"We just need a couple more key investors to get this thing over the line to save the Sydney Kings."

If the pair cannot find the extra cashed-up investors within the next 48 hours, Kordahi and Cousens will recommend the contracted Kings players and coaching staff try to find a spot on other NBL teams. Even if the consortium does raise the money, there is debate about whether the new venture could keep the Sydney Kings name.

We could have invested more ourselves but I wasn't willing to gamble the business I had created on a dream and risk losing it all. Controlled spending and not letting emotions get in the way of business decisions is the most important lesson I learnt from this experience.

Today, the institution that was the Sydney Kings is no more. My dream only lasted one season but even in that short time and despite the sad outcome, I positively influenced a few people's lives along the way.

Of course some were quick to criticise me for having lost money on my dream investment; however, I did secure new business out of my association with the Kings. So from a purely clinical and financial viewpoint, the entire exercise actually turned out to be a good investment in marketing!

Entrepreneurial Strategies – Chapter Nine

- Spend wisely
- Connect (leverage) your networks
- It's okay to have small goals and prepare for the down times
- Tough times call for smart measures

Spend wisely

One of my main business rules is to spend only to a point where you're not exposing yourself. Also, make sure that, when you do spend, you can leverage off it. Prepare for the down times by not spending all your money, which is why I've always believed in running a tight ship. When you run a tight ship, you have good cash flow. Then, if an economic tidal wave hits, you have the resources to overcome these hurdles.

When we experienced the recent global financial crisis, our business was relatively unaffected because our revenue was high. We had sufficient cash flow in the business to sustain us through the tighter periods. When people ask if I have experienced tough times in business, I can honestly state 'no, I haven't', the reason being that I've managed my cash flow well. I've analysed possible risks and I've never exposed the business to a degree that it would be detrimental. By running a tight ship and having good cash flow, I could overcome any hurdle and take on any risk that came my way. And so can you.

Connect (leverage) your networks

Most businesses don't have the brand name to generate significant revenue by cold selling. Therefore, leveraging off your network (or others' networks) to obtain clients is a viable method both beneficial and lucrative. It is critical to build relationships because you never know who knows who or how the dots will connect in a meaningful way for you. Over time, your relationships will generate greater success for you. Most entrepreneurs find their first few clients in this way.

In order to leverage your network, you need to take stock and find out who is in your network. Take the time to see who you know. Chances are you know more people than you realise. As you build relationships with people in your network, make sure that you also open up your network in return. It cannot be one-sided.

Building these relationships is important for several reasons. First, it is a great way to get a referral. In addition, your contacts might also have the inside track on any plans and opportunities within your industry. Remember that your main goal in networking is to learn as much as you can and determine your strengths in your industry.

What do you do if your network does not contain any relevant contacts for your business?

Work out how your networks can cross-pollinate. Remember how I used Cosima to sing at the Sydney Kings games? It attracted celebrity to the basketball scene and increased Cosima's exposure at the same time. Who in your network can be cross-pollinated in this way?

It's okay to have small goals and prepare for the down times

Not every venture you undertake must be a massive step forward. It's okay to take smaller steps, to have smaller goals, as long as you continue to move forward. With the Sydney Kings, my investment in the club didn't return any monetary value, but in terms of exposure of the DKM brand it sure did. I would have loved if it developed into success for the team; however kicking some small goals is still satisfying.

If your venture misses even the smaller goals you set, there are ways to be prepared:

1. Don't panic. Panic gets you nowhere.
2. Keep learning. Learning from the bad times enables you to react quickly when a negative circumstance reoccurs.
3. Realise that it is just money. When a crisis hits, shift your perspective towards the positive things in your life.

The sun will still rise tomorrow. No crisis lasts forever.

Tough times call for smart measures

The state of the economy affects how much companies spend on marketing. For example, if the Australian dollar slides 35 percent, it means that a company's annual spend, if $100,000 dollars one year, is going to cost $135,000 the next.

In tough times many marketing managers will be faced with cuts. But smart companies increase their budgets at that point. It's tough to plan. Why? Because decisions must be made in the harsh light of looking forward. It is much easier to make a reactive decision than a proactive one. During an economic downturn you will hear the words, "Sorry, there's nothing I can do about it. It's just the downturn".

Yet, positioning your company and brand correctly in hard times can be the most profitable thing you can do, both in awareness and market share. Start forging strategic alliances with suppliers and customers alike. This will give you time to plan and budget effectively.

Customers and suppliers alike should be viewed as a long-term commitment. Giving your customers good value for money allows them to better use their budgets to get 'more bang for their buck'.

Notes

Chapter Ten

WHAT I'VE LEARNT ABOUT MERCHANDISING

My hope is that by the time you have finished reading this book, you will have recognised that there are four keys to success in any business: image, perception, differentiation and a point of difference.

Now I don't want this chapter to sound like a sales pitch, but I think it is important to realise that my success has stemmed from doing something against the grain and something that I believed in wholeheartedly. So, I want to reiterate where the promotional products business stood and how my vision differed from the existing view. Hopefully, you can use this knowledge when thinking about your own business plans.

Eight years ago, the promotional products and merchandising industry sat firmly at the bottom end of the marketing industry. It was all about cheap coffee cups, cheap water bottles and cheap t-shirts.

When running an event or a campaign, promotional product purchases were left to the last minute, designed solely to soak up excess marketing budget, assuming there was any. Purchasing decisions were left to the junior office assistants who rang around for three quotes and went with the cheapest.

The approach resulted in the unfortunate association, in the minds of prospects and clients, of valuable corporate brands with products that not only looked cheap but were cheap.

The focus on cheap products reaffirmed the perception that the promotional products industry sat solidly at the low end of the marketing profession. It was a self-perpetuating belief that persisted for decades, right through the 1960s, '70s, '80s and '90s.

This perception has now begun to shift, on the back of some great ideas, and plain hard work, both of which have gone into recent campaigns and produced extraordinary results. There is a new professionalism and a new creativity emerging.

Marketers are beginning to comprehend the strategic value of promotions and merchandising. In turn, promotional product agencies are responding by offering a more sophisticated level of service and output.

Suppliers are increasingly aware of their role in designing and supplying high-value brand platforms, as opposed to simply shipping container loads of cheap product in from China.

Take the sensational Boonie Doll campaign, for example. In case you missed it, the Boonie Doll was part

Chapter Ten | What I've learnt about merchandising

of a Victoria Bitter (VB) campaign. Offered for sale with a carton of beer was a talking David Boon figurine that uttered comments when prompted by cricket's television commentary. We're talking about a very sophisticated product, not just due to the computer chips and timing devices.

The Boonie Doll is an ideal example of how to use a brand platform successfully. It captured perfectly the essence of the VB brand and delivered it into the hands and homes of beer drinkers everywhere. The publicity was astounding. The Boonie Doll will be remembered long after the TV ads and key sponsors are forgotten.

But remnants of the old world persist.

Recently, we at DKM received a phone call from the organisers of a major sporting event. The event was on a Sunday night. The phone call came in on the preceding Wednesday. To ensure the atmosphere was well and truly pumped, the event organisers wanted to hand out a free, promotional product as the crowd entered the stadium. We delivered. (We always do!)

What they got from us was a pretty standard giveaway for sporting events of all codes and significance. But you have to shake your head and wonder, what if they had taken a strategic approach and contacted us weeks earlier? What if, given a little more time and thought, they had been able to give away an item that was unique, that captured the essence of their particular sport? One that people would keep and value?

It wouldn't have cost them extra. But it would have delivered a real punch that had life above and beyond the event itself — just as the Boonie Doll did for VB as well as cricket in general.

I believe the brand platform business delivers great value to consumers, to marketers, to agencies and to suppliers.

Good quality branding is all the more important today, when many brands exist only in cyberspace or on television. Merchandising and promotional products may be the only time your customers come into physical contact with your brand.

The true value of any promotional idea is equal to the perceived value as seen by your customers. High quality and strong utility are just a portion of the equation. The real value your customers look for is confirmation that their trust in your brand is well placed.

So, let's examine more closely what 'value' is to your customer. What value do your prospective (and existing) clients perceive within your brands, products and services?

Value is the single most important issue in the promotions business. Typically, people want to buy a product that costs as little as possible, but is perceived as high value by their clients. 'Value' is discussed via criteria such as weight (heavy items not made of low quality plastic) or usefulness (will people actually use the object?). Weight and usefulness are two great reasons why the ubiquitous coffee cup often wins the day. It is made of nice heavy ceramics and is useful around the office. The value discussion is often, however, only one-dimensional: "How much value will my prospect perceive this gift has?" A more important question is overlooked: "How will this product impact on the value of my brand?"

In the value stakes, nothing is more important than the value proposition wrapped up in your brand. Does the product add value to your brand? Does it diminish the value of your brand? Does it change the perceived value of your brand? What we can't do is lose sight of the real issue. Promotional products are brand platforms first and promotional gifts second.

Imagine for a moment that you work for a promotional products company. The phone rings. It's a junior marketing assistant. They have some budget left over for a conference and want to price a giveaway. The event is in two weeks. Their intention is to get three quotes and then go with the cheapest. The question you need to ask yourself is, in six months time what is the only physical object your delegates will have to remind them of your conference? The answer is of course the giveaway. Do you want the only lasting memory of your event to be the cheapest t-shirt or coffee cup that money can buy? By approaching promotional products differently, as a strategic buy, you can derive an item that is unique, that perfectly encapsulates your brand or your event, and is of real appeal and value to your target audience.

What you are buying, remember, is a platform for your brand. Yes, to some extent the promotional products industry has perpetuated the common misconception that cheap coffee cups, cheap water bottles and cheap t-shirts was what it was all about. But in a fast-paced digital world, the value of an item that can be held in hand, that can persist over time and can be treasured, is becoming paramount. Promotional products are becoming recognised as a key strategic marketing tool.

Think of the promotional products business as the 'brand platform' business. You have the opportunity to deliver to your customers some fantastic items that reflect your brand values perfectly, ones they will keep and treasure, or you could give them a coffee cup and plastic water bottle for the gym. Which would you choose?

Entrepreneurial Strategies – Chapter Ten

- Brand quality is king
- Don't settle for poor customer service
- Get in early to get results

Brand quality is king

My belief in the value of good quality merchandise is why I continue working to elevate the profile of the industry. My goal is to place the industry front and centre in the marketing strategies of our leading corporations.

Why do I think branding is so important? Brand is arguably the most important asset of most businesses. They spend millions building their brands and rely upon them to help sell their wares. Brands are a useful tool because customers come to trust them as a guarantee of quality, as a guarantee that their expectations will be met and, ideally, exceeded.

That's why promotions and merchandising decision-making is crucial. Make the right choice and your brand reaps the benefits. Make the wrong choice and your reputation may be damaged, possibly irrevocably. Promotions and merchandising are about providing brand platforms — not just products, but ideas and concepts as well.

Within DKM, we have a code: we add value to your brand, we protect your brand, we extend your brand and we build your brand.

DKM's business is based upon working with the client to understand the brand and making recommendations that not only set the business apart, but cut through, reinforce and promote their chosen image.

At the end of the day, what your customers want is reassurance that their growing confidence in your brand is well placed. Your customers want to trust your brand and to do so they must sense the existence of a relationship between you.

Don't settle for poor customer service

At DKM, great advice is an integral part of the customer service package. More than just a purveyor of promotional merchandise, DKM is a valuable contributor to its clients' business, providing consultation services to achieve the best possible result for their brands. DKM is all about protecting and enhancing brands through strong management and smart merchandising, as well as providing great service and competitive prices.

The other key value is how the company makes a client feel. It's called good, old-fashioned customer service. And, believe me, it is invaluable.

Every business gives lip service to customer service: "Yes, yes," they say, "customer service is very important." But do they really believe it enough to commit to it fully? If they don't really believe it, perhaps it is because they don't fully understand the reasons behind why customer service is critical.

Let's look at some everyday examples. Telephone a large corporation, utility or finance company. You will be connected to their call processing system and asked to make selections in up to four menu systems. You will hear messages played, telling you to continue holding, the recorded voice repeating that your call is important to them and how much they value your time. Really? Whose time do they actually value?

Call processing menus are designed to cut a company's costs by increasing call centre efficiency. Today, call centre staff earn about $20 an hour. Therefore, the call centre values your time at a rate of less than $20 an hour; otherwise they would scrap the efficiency methods in favour of improving service levels. But it is not just large corporations that offer a minimum of service. Many ultramodern internet businesses are just as bad, offering no more than an email customer service or complaint option, to a general recipient, such as info@acme.com.au. When you get a response, how many times is it a computer-generated response rather than a personal response by a specific employee? You may wonder then, does customer service really matter all that much? Many companies appear to thrive despite offering terrible service.

In my business, the customer service philosophy is to provide not only a fast turnaround but take the time to understand the customer and what works for their business. I differentiated my business by putting an end to handing the customer a catalogue of standard, cheap (i.e., low value) promotional items. Make it your business truly to understand your customer and provide exceptional service.

Get in early to get results

In contrast to the temporary and costly nature of media campaigns, a good below the line campaign can deliver cost-effective items directly into your target market and leave your customer with a lasting reminder of your brand. But don't leave the details to the last minute. A good promotional merchandise company is every bit as creative as above the line agencies. You can't, however, expect to call a promotional products company on behalf of an event that's taking place in just three days time and still get an exceptional creative product. You must learn how to use the services of promotional product companies effectively. Promotional products can be innovative, fun and memorable; they can really drive a campaign when done properly.

Placing your brand on items with a high perceived value reflects that you care about both your customer and your brand, by offering them something worth keeping and using for a long time to come. Every time they use that product they will be favourably reminded of your brand.

Quality does not necessarily translate to costly, but items, whether large or small, should be well designed and well manufactured. Perception is a very important part of delivering a great product campaign — it adds value.

Notes

Chapter Eleven

THE POWER OF POSITIVE THINKING

Life is amazing. We often wonder what our purpose on this earth is, what makes us tick and what makes some people get ahead in life. Is it our will, our inner belief, sheer luck, our self-dependence? The universe is a big place and from a distance we appear no more than little ants running around trying to find our way.

My friends ask, "How the hell do things just happen for you?" When I watched the so-called secrets in *The Secret*, it became obvious to me that this secret was something I'd been intuitively applying throughout my life.

The Secret says if you believe in something, even just subconsciously, it will happen. Well, it's not a secret anymore. In fact, I want everyone to realise and believe that if I can do it, anyone can.

I have never been a big reader of autobiographies or business books until someone gave me a copy of Richard Branson's *Losing My Virginity*. I devoured that book from cover to cover. I was mesmerised. This entrepreneur, famous for his global success and cosmic vision, began his business, his dream, with the same mental approach I had. Although my success is hardly at the level of the multi-layered, billionaire, high profile achievements of Sir Richard, the fact is that young Mr Branson began his empire based on a business plan scribbled on scraps of paper. My own original business plan scraps of paper remain to this day locked away safely, a reminder of my humble beginnings. There were no expensive consultants or slick presentations; there were only the handwritten notes of dreams and aspirations penned on bits of paper.

The chances Richard Branson took and how he manoeuvred things in his favour, versus how I have progressed are closer than they may appear. While reading his autobiography, I became even more convinced than ever that I had chosen the right path. I was equally convinced that others who did likewise would also achieve the seemingly impossible.

Some claim you must develop an impressively comprehensive business plan before you can ever get ahead. Frankly, that's bullshit. Remember what I told you. Keep it simple. Reading *Losing My Virginity* reaffirmed that.

Seeing the big picture is akin to seeing a huge, flashing neon sign. Too often, though, our blinkered conditioning prevents us from seeing the obvious. Sometimes I have difficulty explaining this. To me it is so clear but others can't always see what I'm seeing.

Chapter Eleven | **The Power of Positive Thinking**

Someone pointed out to me once that if everyone could see what I see, then no one would ever shine above the rest because everyone would be shining. There cannot be leaders without followers and there will always be followers — no amount of inspiration or education will ever change that. I have always deliberately sought out people who were more successful than I to mix with and learn from. If you are to be a leader, hoping to aspire to great heights, you must prepare yourself psychologically for how your life will change as a result.

If you're successful at what you do, you will find you lose friends. Those you gain may often be for the wrong reasons. I have fewer friends nowadays but more acquaintances. I anticipated that. It's part of being mentally prepared for success.

You must also be sensible and not get carried away with your newfound wealth, blowing it away on frivolous luxuries or destructive lifestyles, or expanding your business too fast in a desperate attempt to gain every inch you can. If you do, you may find you lose everything you've built up far faster than you acquired it. I've seen too many people rise to success without being mentally equipped for it, only to find they are broke soon after.

There's also the 'tall poppy' syndrome, where, as soon as you poke your head up, someone, somewhere, will try to chop it off.

We hear so often of fast-rising celebrities who resort to self-destructive behaviour such as drugs, as a coping mechanism. That lack of preparation for all the facets of success means they've failed to stay grounded. As soon as they scale the mountain, they find themselves falling off the peak.

Failure can be an important lesson, too, but it makes sense to avoid it if you can. I don't believe you need to go bankrupt first in order to learn how to succeed. I'd rather learn my lesson from observing other people's mistakes, not making my own.

I'm not saying I don't make mistakes. Far from it. I've made my fair share. There will always be circumstances you cannot control, but where things that happen around you and to you are within the realm of your control, there is no real excuse for failure. When going into a situation where a risk factor is evident, I plan ahead to minimise any possible negative exposure.

Risk management aside, it's inevitable that people's attitudes towards you will change once you start to shine. When this happens, take it as a sign that you are on the right track. I've been told I changed as I became successful. I disagree. I'm still the same person. It is the other person's perception of me that has changed.

Every successful person has had ups and downs. Preparing for the down times, minor or major, is simply a matter of training one's mind to find the positive in any situation. It's said, if someone offers you a lemon, make lemonade. Most negatives, whether they are your state of mind or a bad situation in which you find yourself, can be inverted and viewed as a positive if you train your mind to automatically look for the silver lining surrounding the dark, threatening cloud. Visualisations were once scoffed upon but this technique is not only widely accepted now but is becoming a standard tool. It costs nothing and is accessible to everyone; you just have to train yourself to do it.

Even if you have a natural aptitude for visualisation, you must still train yourself to do it effectively. Pianists may be born with natural ability but that does not mean they are automatically at concert-level performance. They must practise, practise, practise, to achieve mastery. And so it is with all aspects of life. The moment you stop learning is the moment you die.

How much has visualisation contributed to my success? It's hard to gauge but I know one thing for certain — it definitely helped!

When you train yourself to think positively, you have the potential to change not only your own life around but the lives of those around you, sometimes without even realising it at the time. By believing in myself, overcoming obstacles and using positive visualisation, I set out on the right path without ever consciously deciding to do so.

It is exciting to see people take that first step to improve themselves. That first step is unquestionably the hardest. And when you see someone doing that, you react naturally by wanting to help them, because you sense they're eager to learn. The choice is yours. If you don't choose to do it for yourself, no one can make you do it. Choosing to do so, though and helping others to do so as well, is enormously rewarding.

Things haven't always been rosy for me. In my early 20s, it was tough feeling I wasn't getting anywhere. I was on the unemployment benefit for a year because there was no income within the business. Being forced to live on $100 a week at 22 years of age, when my friends were earning far more money and were able to do and buy things that I couldn't was very dispiriting. I had my basketball, which brought me great joy but no income. Even to go out for a drink with my mates was a challenge. I'd make a quick buck here and there, buying something and reselling it but I feared I would never get ahead. I wondered how I would ever be able to afford a home of my own.

The turning point was changing my way of thinking. Instead of thinking about the money, I began thinking of building the right belief system, of building the right model and that the money would come if I focused on finding my niche, my passion. When I began my company, I didn't focus on the money aspect; I focused on building the right values for the business and the right model.

I am an optimist by nature. I have always believed in myself intrinsically. But there will always be dark moments, no matter how positive I am. The key is to accept that and move on.

It is how you bounce yourself out of despair that counts. It requires willpower and a 'can do' attitude, something you can build in yourself without any tool other than willingness. Don't be a quitter. Don't be prepared to lose. If you suffer low self-esteem or if you don't have strong willpower and you don't make an effort to change, if instead you just keep on doing what you've always done, then you'll never have more than you have right now. To change your life you need to change yourself. It is a discipline. Remember how we talked about 'just fake it 'til you make it?' Every day, consciously focus on what is positive in your life. Count your blessings, literally, however basic they may be. Make a list and reread it when you feel a weak moment coming on. Do you have a roof over your head? Food on the table? Your health? A loving family? Good friends? You might be surprised at how long this list actually is. And once you've tallied up those blessings, say a thank you for each and every one of them. Do this for a few minutes every day. Gratitude actually lifts your spirits.

I drove a beat-up van to work every morning because that was all I could afford. It wasn't exactly a chick magnet; I was too embarrassed to even drive it to a club or into the city. Those times make you appreciate the good times.

Reaching an undeniable level of success does not protect you from those dark moments. The sun still throws dark shadows on occasion. Sometimes I feel sad that I seem to have few real friends and that those around me may be there for selfish reasons.

When I do, I'll take some time to myself. Alone time helps me. We can't always be on a high; everything doesn't go right all of the time. Life isn't perfect. But there is an advantage in knowing that, when we're feeling down, it can actually be a healthy way to re-establish balance. That's what I meant about finding the silver lining, no matter what. If life was a constant high, we would never appreciate the good times. To cherish the highs, you must suffer the lows. The trick is to know how to pull yourself out of a gloomy patch. If you hit rock bottom, the only other direction to go is up!

My brother, Danny and I have now merged our companies to create DKM Blue. Earlier in our careers, we followed different paths. I focused on China for my importing and on brand management. Danny focused on online ordering systems and corporate uniforms. In merging our businesses, we cut overheads and became joint CEOs, each managing the different areas of the merged operation. As children, we were both very competitive. Today, we have matured and look forward to a bright future together, taking DKM Blue to where no merchandising and marketing company has gone before.

I hope that, after reading this book, you will be both inspired and motivated to be the best you can be. Where there's a will, there's a way.

Chapter Eleven | The Power of Positive Thinking

If you believe in yourself and act on those beliefs, you can achieve any goal you choose. There is no right or wrong; it is about what's right for you. It is what you believe that's important. There are no set guidelines or ingredients for success. Just believe and take that first step.

As I said in the very first chapter, you don't land on a mountain; you climb a mountain. Every day will be a climb. Some days will be easy; some days will be tough.

Some days the climb is going to be steep and you'll feel exhausted. You'll want to give up. But, if you quit, you'll spend the rest of your life wondering *what if?* If you believe you'll succeed, you will. If you believe you'll fail — you will. You must fight for what you believe in and keep on fighting. If you want to be a follower, someone else's employee, all your life, that's OK. But I doubt you'd be reading this book if you did. Don't despair if you see your peers climbing the ladder, be it life or career and leaving you behind. It's an excellent time to pause and assess. Take a hard look at why you feel like you're standing still. Step out of your comfort zone and start climbing!

Within each of us lies the *power to act*, personally, professionally and emotionally. Never stop learning and never stop setting new goals.

I hope some of the lessons I've learned on the way will empower you on your own journey.

If you think it will take luck instead of willingness, think about this:

- If you have luck, it won't help you unless you know what to do with it.

- If you get an opportunity, you need to know how to leverage off it.

- If you make money, you need to know how to spend wisely.

- If you have a dream, you need to know how to make it a reality.

Now it is up to you.
Find within yourself, today, the

"*Power to Act!*"